Lomzo, Poland; June 1991

i

During travels in 1993

ii

PRIEST OF THE WORLD'S DESTINY: JOHN PAUL II

Sabina, Italy; March 1993

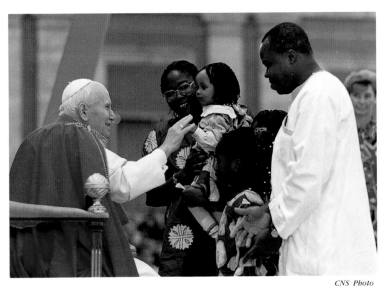

Family Festival, Vatican City; Fall of 1994

Denver, Colorado, USA; August 1993

Denver, Colorado, USA;
August 1993

Denver, Colorado, USA;
August 1993

PRIEST OF THE WORLD'S DESTINY: JOHN PAUL II

by
Michael Parker

Published by:
Faith Publishing Company
P.O. Box 237
Milford, OH 45150

The publisher recognizes and accepts that the final authority regarding apparitions and private revelation rests with the Holy See of Rome, to whose judgment we willingly submit.

—The Publisher

This book is an updated version of *This Portentous Priest*, which was originally published in 1986 by The Tauranga Moana Press of Tauranga, New Zealand (ISBN 0-908705-12-3). Faith Publishing Company is pleased to publish it with the written understanding that the author holds absolute copyright to its contents.

Published by: Faith Publishing Company
P.O. Box 237
Milford, OH 45150-0237
USA

Additional copies of this book may be acquired by contacting:

For book stores: Faith Publishing Company
P.O. Box 237
Milford, OH 45150-0237
USA
Phone: 1-800-576-6477 or
1-513-576-6400
Fax: 1-513-576-0022

For individuals: The Riehle Foundation
P.O. Box 7
Milford, OH 45150-0007
USA
Phone: 1-513-576-0032

FRONT COVER PHOTO CREDIT: (Zagreb, Croatia; 1994) CNS Photo

BACK COVER PHOTO CREDIT: (Denver, Colorado, USA; August 1993) CNS Photo

With American Bishops; Vatican City; October 13, 1993

With Orthodox Leaders; Bialystok, Poland; June 1991

Table of Contents

With a Sick Patient and Mother Teresa's Missionaries
of Charity; Jamaica; August 1993

With President Bill Clinton; Denver, Colorado, USA;
August 1993

Foreword

The jury of the general populace is still out, but many people who study world events from a religious perspective predict that, some day, history will portray our present Holy Father, Pope John Paul II, as the greatest person to have lived during the 20th Century. No one can ever truthfully deny this one man's contribution to mankind. His love for Our Lord and our Blessed Mother radiates through his words and his entire being. His love for all people, regardless of age, race, gender, nationality, or even religious belief or non-belief is evident through his many pilgrimages into virtually every land on earth. His profound intellect is reflected in his prolific writings and homilies. His goodness is demonstrated in his perseverance and devotion to prayer.

He is a student of the world and a teacher of its inhabitants. He is a devoted son of Poland and a citizen of the entire world. He is a faithful lamb of Jesus and a loyal shepherd to Jesus' flock. He is the pinpoint beam of light which directs our attention to the one true Light of the World, Jesus Christ. He is humble before God and humanity but intensely proud in his faith.

As he draws crowds numbering in the millions with his charismatic personality, it is the substance of his speech which puts off his detractors. He is a threat. He understands and communicates, perhaps better than anyone else alive today, the interrelationships between people, communities, nations, and their God. He "gets the big picture." He exposes and manipulates the world's evils, in more dynamic and climactic ways than have ever been tried before—that they be destroyed. He is an appropriate conduit for the power of God.

Those who love him love him intensely; they know his heart is with God. Those who oppose him fail to acknowledge the depth of Pope John Paul's perception and conviction. He has admirers and disparagers. But one thing is sure—no one can be indifferent to him.

Michael Parker has succeeded in putting together a verbal portrait of this great man who is so human, yet so much the Vicar (face) of Christ—a holy pope. Mr. Parker has woven a rich tapestry of love and war, personal biography and world history, secular philosophy and Catholic theology, warmth and intrigue, which is sure to swell the hearts of all people who love our present pontiff. We are proud to publish this work as a testimony to our devotion to our Holy Father and his teachings. May this book and Pope John Paul II lead many souls to the Truth Who is Jesus Christ!

—Laurie Balbach-Taylor
Faith Publishing Company

*   *   *

Michael Parker is a freelance journalist and writer, of orthodox Roman Catholic background, who resides in the beautiful pastoral province of Hawke's Bay in New Zealand.

His journalistic career has included 10 years' employment with the reporting staffs of several daily newspapers, among them the morning paper of his country's capital city, Wellington.

Mr. Parker has written positively on religious matters for several New Zealand and Australian Catholic journals, and has also tried to raise the profile of two outstanding religious in the history of his national Church. Although New Zealand has had the faith for more than one and a half centuries, the country still has no indigenous canonized saint.

His first book, written 15 years ago, was a history of the NZ Security Intelligence Service, his country's equivalent of Britain's MI5. A *cause celebre* arose over his exposure of a leading KGB official at the Soviet Union's Wellington embassy, the embassy's denial of the official's status, and the author's subsequent revelation of some of the man's foreign career activities.

Michael was involved in a small way during the 1980s in support of Soviet political religious prisoners.

He is reasonably well traveled, and lived in England for several years. He was able to spend some time in Rome in 1984, to learn more about the papacy.

His education included several years in the Hawke's Bay seminary of a religious order, and he claims "two thirds of a Bachelor of Theology degree."

It was, first, Michael's love of sports, and interest in Soviet and East European history, that helped propel his attraction to the Pole Karol Wojtyla in 1978. "Sports are a principal part of my country's culture, and with my previously having known only anemic Italian popes aged in their 70s and 80s, the new Pope's strong liking for and active participation in several sports made a considerable impact on me.

"Wojtyla's religious poetry, as I came to learn of it and read it, was also an attraction. I had just spent an English winter in a village in Devonshire on the edge of the moors trying to write an epic verse play.

"When I read his complex work of philosophy, *The Acting Person*, I was astonished at the Pope's shrewd understanding of secular democracy and the pertinence of his commentary that all adult citizens must actively participate in the decision making process of government.

"Then came the epochal Solidarity events in Poland, to which he gave leadership. The 1981 assassination attempt marked him for me as the Pope of Fatima, and I began to write professionally about him as the Polish Peter and the great Marian pope promised for the world by the Blessed Virgin in 1917." These writings culminated in Michael's new book published now by Faith Publishing Company.

Michael is a lay leader in his parish of St. Patrick in Napier city, and a special Minister of the Eucharist on behalf of his city's three parishes to Catholic patients in Napier Public Hospital. As an active member of a Medjugorje prayer group, he helped prepare a nine-week Marian novena last year in his parish for Hawke's Bay Catholics, in the style of the great Marian novenas of the 1950s.

Manila, Philippines; 1994

Dedication

To Joan R.
With my love and thanks for all.

Author's Note

I express my appreciation to D. Reidel Publishing Company of Dordrecht, Holland, publishers of *The Acting Person*, for permission to quote from that book to the extent that I have. The publishers asked me to make special mention of the book's editor, Professor Anna-Teresa Tymieniecka of Boston.

I would like it known that, while I have met the Pope, he was not a subject of interview for this book. After my extensive research and work, there remained outstanding several intimacies which I knew in advance John Paul would not speak to for the record.

To all those who have assisted me in this profile I thank you from my heart.

I wish to thank in particular at Faith Publishing Company, Mrs. Laurie Balbach-Taylor whose good sense and enthusiasm was of much help in forming my manuscript. She is the manuscript's editor.

Though Karol Wojtyla has trod the globe's stage for almost 17 years now as Pope John Paul II, there is much in this manuscript that is new about a man whom I regard as the world's most important.

Michael Parker
Hawke's Bay, New Zealand
March 1995

Chapter 1

Of and To Poland

"Before I leave you, I wish to give one more look at Cracow, this Cracow in which every stone and every brick is dear to me...."

Such emotional attachment to a city was evocative of a bygone age, and the words might have been unheard, their author unknown, had not the speaker and his day been made so visible and audible by modern technology.

"And I look once more on my Poland."

Beyond his beloved city he was departing his homeland, and the word "my," singular in its proclamation, made the speaker special.

"You must be strong, dear brothers and sisters. You must be strong with the strength of faith. I beg you, never lose your trust, do not be defeated, do not be discouraged, do not on your own cut yourselves off from the roots from which we had our origins. Never lose your spiritual freedom. I beg you."

The amplified, rich voice fell silent—yet the television and film cameras still bore upon his Slavic countenance. From the high podium on which he stood he irresistibly lifted his blue eyes again over the faces of two million people spread before him across the green freshness of great Blonie Park meadow to the grey and brown brick and stone

1

architecture of his Cracow, made resilient and resonant through seven centuries.

He had been in Cracow four days. Two mornings after his arrival he had awoken at 4 a.m. Not able to return to sleep he had dressed and, incognito, walked about the city, cradle of Polish culture and history, past Gothic and baroque churches, the Jagiellonian University, monastic buildings, the Renaissance courtyards, across the magnificent main market square centered by the bister Town Hall tower.

Here had been made the shape and heart of him. This city had been his in a way only a Pole really understood, for while alien dictatorial communism was the land's temporal power, Roman Catholicism remained the impetus of the people's constancy and nationalism, and he had risen to be Archbishop of Cracow. He was theirs, and this city's people were his.

When last he had walked these streets and squares, eight months ago, he was Karol Cardinal Wojtyla. Now, after a Cardinal's College exclamation unique in history, he was Pope John Paul II, the first Polish, first Slav pope.

The papacy, in giving this Pole the spiritual and moral leadership of 840 million Roman Catholics around the globe, had made him the world's most prominent churchman. That it had taken away Poland from him had greatly distressed him on the October 16, 1978, evening of his election as the "Polish Peter." Plaintively, he had placed a long-distance telephone call to a priest friend in Poland: "I'm calling because I feel a little lonely. I'm sad without my friends. How are things in Cracow?"

In another telephone call, to a nun who had served him in Cracow's old Episcopal Palace on Franciszkanska Street, his first words had been simply: "It's me."

To a Polish friend who had come into the Vatican's private offices the day after the election to offer congratulations, Wojtyla had asked quietly: "How can I leave all those six hundred priests I have ordained back home?" And the new Pope had broken down and cried.

For Cracovians their first reaction to the news of their Lolek's (a diminutive form of Karol) election had been astonishment. Then had come unrestrained rejoicing, and

then the painful realization that the world's gain was to
be their great loss.

With a quickness demonstrating his love of country, John
Paul had physically clasped the communion of his countrymen to him in an emotional audience for Polish pilgrims
in the Sala Nervi of the Vatican the first day after his formal
inauguration as Pope. To the several thousand present, led
by the Cardinal Primate of Poland, the Venerable Stefan
Wyszynski, the Pope's opening remarks made vivid the
native well-springs of his mind: "My beloved countrymen,
it has fallen to the lot of a son of our dear motherland to
assume episcopal office as the successor of St. Peter. . . .
The Church in Poland has become an object of great
interest by reason of the conjuncture of circumstances
which is of such importance to the aspirations of contemporary humanity, of so many nations and states. It has
become a Church of especial witness, toward which the
eyes of all the world are turned. Without realizing this fact
it is hard to understand that the Pope who speaks to you
today is a Pole."

So it was that his loss bore down upon him more
severely: "It is not easy to accept the fact that one cannot
return home. . ." [the emotional interchange with his
audience stopped Wojtyla briefly] "but since it is the will
of Christ, I must accept. I ask you that my departure may
unite us more than ever. Do not forget me in your prayers;
I beg you, too, resist anything that impairs human dignity
and lowers the moral health of society."

Letting go of Cracow, though, had been the hardest part:
"Believe me, my beloved Archdiocese of Cracow, when I
came to Rome for the conclave, my greatest desire was to
return to you. Allow me to thank you for all those years
of my life, as a student, priest, and bishop. I think of my
beloved parents, who died long ago, and my primary and
secondary school, and the Jagiellonian University, the
Faculty of Theology, and the Theological Seminary. And
what shall I say of my great predecessor as Archbishop,
Cardinal Prince Adam Sapieha, and all the bishops and
priests and devoted shepherds of souls, the learned profes-
sors and the exemplary monks and nuns?

"What of all the layfolk I have met in the course of my

life, my school friends and fellow students at the university and seminary, the workers at the Solvay plant, the intellectuals, artists and writers, people of all professions, married couples, young people engaged in apostolic and missionary work, and all the young men and women who, with the Gospel in hand, sought the meaning of life, and some of whom finally chose to become priests or enter a religious order? All these I bear in my heart and, in a sense, take with me: the whole of my beloved church in Cracow. . . . May God bless you all! Once again I commend you to Christ through the maternal hands and heart of His blessed Mother.''

John Paul's formal words concluded, but not his leavetaking. For an hour he walked amongst them, stretching out both hands to touch and be touched, to embrace and be embraced. They were Poles together. The preferment of the papacy would never remove the smallest part of Karol Wojtyla's patrimony and patriotism.

Now, eight months later, he had been reunited with his precious Cracovians. His exuberant words on arrival at the city by helicopter were to be expected: "I'm back, my children!"

The Pope had, in fact, wanted to be "back" a month earlier, to celebrate in person the May 8 feast day and 900th anniversary of the death of St. Stanislaus of Szczepanow, Poland's patron saint. (Elaborate preparations for the anniversary's celebrations had been put in motion by Cardinal Wojtyla himself early in 1978.) St. Stanislaus had been martyred in 1079 at the hands of King Boleslaus the Bold for his assertion of the inalienable right of the individual to criticize those in authority. The saint, too, had been an Archbishop—his remains lie in Cracow's Wawel Cathedral—and many times from Wawel Cathedral's pulpit, Wojtyla in his archbishop's attire had reached back almost nine centuries to venerate and do homage to the martyr. For a regime whose voracious censorship had been a pillar of its rule, the symbolism would be too much.

From the first intimation—soon after his inauguration—of John Paul's natural impulse for a reunion with his homeland, the psychology had been awry: atheistic communists, pretenders of the people's interests in a nation that was 90 percent Roman Catholic, having to welcome back a native son whose apolitical and apostolic office would command the affections of Poles in a concord no communist could compete with. He was, too, a man of such intellect—Doctor of Divinity at the age of 28, lecturer on social ethics at Cracow Theological Seminary at the age of 33, a Professor and head of the Institute of Ethics in Lublin Catholic University at the age of 36—that as both priest and democrat he had easily bested the Marxist theorists in argument. No, the regime would not embarrass itself by having Wojtyla back in May to celebrate that particular anniversary. The new Pope could come in June, the regime said.

That modification of course did not moderate his triumph. Here were a people whose Catholicism is probably the most profound in the world, and certainly the inspiration of their nationhood, meeting with the first Pope to visit Poland. That this Pope's journey was a pilgrimage to the genesis of his consummate faith in and love of God made for no boundary of brotherhood, happiness, and accomplishment.

"I greet you in the name of Christ, as I learned to greet people here in Poland.

"—in Poland, my native land, to which I remain deeply attached by the roots of my life, of my heart, of my vocation.

"—in Poland, this country in which, as the poet Cyprian Norwid wrote, 'people gather up, through respect for Heaven's gifts, every crumb that falls to the ground'; where the first greeting is the eternal confession of Christ: Praised be Jesus Christ!

"—in Poland, which throughout the course of its thousand year history has been linked with the Church of Christ and the See of Rome by a special bond of spiritual unity.

"Beloved brothers and sisters, fellow countrymen, I am coming to you as a son of this land, of this nation, and also, by the inscrutable designs of Providence, as a successor of St. Peter in the See of Rome. I thank you for inviting me. I greet in spirit and embrace with my heart every human being living in the land of Poland."

Sensitive to the situation of his presence, the Pope's homage to his homeland on arrival by air in Warsaw from

Rome on June 2 emphasized that his was a religious and pastoral visit.

Gleaming in a white cassock, John Paul, on alighting from his Alitalia aircraft, first kissed the ground of Poland. But then came a surprise. The President of Poland, Henryk Jablonski, of course a communist, spoke in genuine warmth of "the exceptional character of this grand moment and its meaning." Several times Jablonski used the term "your Holiness." The Pope was visibly moved by this generous official greeting.

Then they came to him in their millions:

—to this Pole who had philosophized a dimension of divinity in man made by God, which dignified our humanity and was the conduit for man's ethical action and freedom;

—to this Pole who apprehended in each individual the greatest worth, which was the commonalty of man and Christ;

—to this Pole whose inspirational sense of community had made him a magnetic priest and pastor.

For nine brief days Karol Wojtyla was again all theirs. In Warsaw, Wadowice, Czestochowa, Cracow, and more, adorned with banners and flags of the papal colors of yellow and white, they prayed with him, cheered him, and listened to him. Over twelve million of them.

In every place he went he emphasized the two towers of spiritual strength: Jesus Christ and the Virgin Mary. An emphasis, he knew, that had an inner challenge to communism. "Man cannot be fully understood without Christ," the Pope said in Victory Square, Warsaw, before a towering wooden cross and altar erected for the occasion. "Nor can man fully understand himself without Christ. He cannot understand who he is, nor what his true dignity is, nor what his vocation is, nor what his final end is. He cannot understand any of this without Christ.

"Therefore, Christ cannot be kept out of the history of man in any part of the globe, at any longitude or latitude of geography. The exclusion of Christ from the history of man is an act against man. Without Christ it is impossible to understand the history of Poland, especially the history of the people who have passed or are passing through this land."

To the university students of Warsaw, the next day, he posed, "...the fundamental query for man: 'Who am I?' What is to be the measurement for measuring man? That of the physical forces at his command? That of the senses that enable him to have contact with the external world? Or that of the intelligence obtained by means of the various tests or examinations? Today's answer points to two measurements: Man must be measured by the measurement of his 'heart.' In biblical language the heart means the inner spirituality of man; in particular, it means conscience. Man must therefore be measured by the measurement of conscience, by the measurement of the spirit open to God. Only the Holy Spirit can 'fill' this heart, that is to say, lead it to self-realization through love and wisdom."

The relationship the Poles have with the Virgin Mary is unique. Our Lady is "Queen of Poland," a position temporal in sound and stimulation, as well as spiritual, to the discomfort of the regime. She is also a personal passion of the Pope, the Mother of his Church. Before *The Black Madonna* (a painting of Our Lady holding her son the Christ, its artistry attributed by legend to the evangelist St. Luke, and Poland's most sacred relic) in the Paulite monastery of Jasna Gora overlooking the town of Czestochowa, John Paul said with emotion: "How meaningful for me always have been the words that your Son, born from you, Jesus Christ, the Redeemer of Man, spoke from the height of the Cross, pointing to John the Apostle: *'Woman, behold, your son!'* In these words I have always found the place for every human being and the place for myself."

As he left Jasna Gora after two days he exclaimed: "Mother of the Church! I consecrate to you humanity; I consecrate to you all men and women, my brothers and sisters. All the peoples and the nations, I consecrate to you Europe and all the continents. Mother, accept us! Mother, do not abandon us! Mother, be our guide!"

And finally came Cracow, as it had to come. Together, the Pope wiping a tear, and his last vast congregation, at Blonie Park meadow, had sung the hauntingly beautiful mountaineer's ballad: "O highlander, do you not grieve for the land that gave you birth, for the forests of spruce and

the meadows, and the streams of running silver? O highlander, do you not grieve?''

Then the man Wojtyla was taking one more look at his
Cracow, then pleading with them all: ''You must be strong,
dear brothers and sisters. You must be strong with the
strength that comes from faith.''

As the LOT Polish aircraft which carried him away from
Cracow touched down at Rome, Poland's government-
controlled press commented approvingly of the ''discipline
of the faithful'' and the ''good co-operation between the
state and Church authorities.'' The following day, the Polish Foreign Ministry's chief spokesman declared his
government to have been ''deeply satisfied with the course
of the Holy Father's visit.''

All seemed propitious for the Pontiff to re-visit his homeland. This, most media commentators from the West
agreed, would be just over three years hence, in August
1982, for the Marian 600th anniversary of the installation
of *The Black Madonna* painting at Jasna Gora. John Paul
had already joined the Polish faithful to this thought, and
at Jasna Gora. The Prefect of the Pontifical Household and
the Chief of Vatican Protocol are officials who must travel
with the Pope. ''They are novices in Poland,'' he told a
large gathering around the monastery, ''but they will get
used to it,'' he quipped, demonstrating his humor and his
desire to frequently re-visit his homeland.

Chapter 2

Three Polish Proportions

It was August 15, 1982. Some 350,000 worshippers had gathered upon the ramparts of Jasna Gora monastery in the transcendent celebration of the 600th anniversary of *The Black Madonna* shrine. From a high balcony, a new Primate of Poland, Archbishop Jozef Glemp, opened his arms above their heads. Beside him on the balcony was a papal chair, empty.

For Poles, there could not have been a more somber and stark contrast to what had been, than that their own Pastor could not come to comfort them, that their Pope had been kept from speaking to them and blessing them in this great Catholic and national celebration, a commemoration he had so dearly wished to join there at Jasna Gora.

The lines of suffering on John Paul's face were evident as he listened, in his Castel Gandolfo summer residence outside Rome, to reports of the Jasna Gora rites.

More poignant than the plaintive telephone calls to Poland, after his election, had been what he said in his homily during his formal installation as Pope, six days later, when he quoted Christ to Peter, while all Poland knew it to be an ironic, personal insight: *"When you were young you put on your own belt and walked where you liked; but when you grow old you will stretch out your hands and somebody else will put a belt around you and*

9

take you where you would rather not go.''

In June 1979, he and his Poles together had shared the most joyful celebration of Christ's being and values. He had been so carried by this communion with his beloved Cracow that, as he knelt before his family's grave in the city, he had revealed a family member unknown to the public, unknown even to his close friends: "I have a sister." The girl had been born to his parents several years before his own birth, but had lived only a day.

Now "they" had closed away his homeland from him, emptied him a whole measure. This while he had still not fully recovered from serious physical wounds.

Nor was unnatural deprivation peculiarly his. Hundreds of Polish patriots and democrats to whom he had given strength now suffered internment.

During that time, just over three years between his papal return home and when he unsuccessfully sought his homeland again, a tide of Poles had realized, and then had had taken from them, the most prolonged and profound movement for and of democracy in the history of communist East Europe, peaceful in its venture, Christian in its values.

As John Paul occupied the trauma now, after the triumph that had so essentially been his own inspiration, the thought that he might not again possess the priceless communion of his countrymen must have borne down upon him.

"Before I leave you, I wish to give one more look at Cracow...."

All knew that the absence of Pope John Paul II from Jasna Gora in August 1982 was due to the word "solidarity," long rich in use in Poland. The campaign named by this word had been fired into a Polish mass movement of defiance and democracy in August 1980. Yet, it was a paradox to ponder that, had Poles not passed through the triumphs and tragedies of 1980-82, had they not created a drama whose audience became the whole world, through sixteen months of piercing light and liberty, the papacy of the Polish Peter would not have had that eclectic and enthralled world audience.

Indeed, it had been uncanny how the unprecedented election of a Pole had gained, again in 1978, the globe's attention for the Roman papacy, and in its wake, that most

Christian of nations, his own Poland, had come from years of relative obscurity to light a lantern of liberty for both east and west, in the most trying of circumstances, and become a dominant thread in the web of world news.

In acknowledgment of this phenomenon, could it not be perceived that, with humanity more disturbed, secular, and dangerous than any part of our history, the three proportions of (1.) Poland's faith, (2.) the Pole who is Pope, and (3.) the Poles' ethical endeavors to be masters of their own destiny came together to form a providential path for us to return to dignity and sanctuary? That it came to be through suffering—Poles sometimes call their country the Christ of nations—heightens the revelatory drama of these events.

The Polish proportions of this whole were magnificent.

1. Poland's Faith

The maxim of faith, a sustained belief in God, is lived to varying commitment and enthusiasm. Faith can be practiced in freedom, or against the dictates of those who hold governmental power. More than 12 million Poles, and as many perhaps as 20 million,[1] came to their Vicar of Christ's Masses and ceremonies during those nine days of June 1979. The multitudes who had met the 1000th year of Christianity in Poland in 1966, with fervent public re-dedications of their devotion, were totally eclipsed.

Though a joyful faith, for forty years it had not been an easy one. First the Nazi occupiers, then the post-War communist regime, maintained by the presence of Soviet arms, knew the Church would be their strongest opponent. During the five years of German occupation, 3600 Polish priests were imprisoned in concentration camps (all but 1000 of whom died there), along with seven bishops (four of whom died there). After the "liberation" of 1945, there was no relief. The new, atheistic communist dictators determined to complete the destruction of the Church. By 1952, 1000 priests had been cast into Siberian and Polish prisons. In 1953, eight bishops and the Primate himself, Cardinal Wyszynski, were seized. Late in 1956, though, leaders of the regime looked across at the Hungarian revo-

---

1. The population of Poland is 37 million.

lution, and released the many imprisoned Polish clergy. But the regime continued to press down upon the Church with a vigor which, while short of imprisonment, was still intent on religion's destruction.

Certainly since 1939, no people have suffered more for their Christianity than the Poles. Yet those who have suffered the most know God the best. And the loyalty which they gave and which was given in return, made, in that June of 1979, the most effusive affirmation of Christian allegiance and trust since A.D. 33. You can go right back through the annals of Christianity. You will not find, since that unparagoned act of Death and Resurrection, a greater number of Christians joining with their Pope in indomitable and joyful exaltation of their faith than did those many millions of Poles with their Polish Peter. That ennobling and exuberant spirituality was an eloquent answer to the complaints of the Christian West that the precepts and duties of its faith are onerous.

2. The Pole Who Is Pope

The man Karol Wojtyla grew from this constant Polish faith, yet his mind has made its own path. English Archbishop Derek Worlock of Liverpool has said Wojtyla "has the greatest intellect I have ever met," a statement without religious overtone or qualification. Indeed, this particular Pole's philosophical writings on solidarity and individual ethics have furthered the concept of secular democracy. That can only come from a man who has been much in contact with people's daily lives. That this person is also a priest, so often possessed of prayer and probably closer to God than any living soul, gives a start to understanding the dimensions of the man.

Wojtyla has been termed by those who know him well—and there are many who know him well—a mystic. William James, in his Gifford lectures of 1901-2, presented a keen insight of the mystic. Mystical experiences, James said, delved into "the depths of truth unplumbed by the discursive intellect," and gave "knowledge of God beyond the ordinary powers of the intellect." The experiences last a short time, and "the mystic feels as if his own will is in abeyance, and indeed sometimes as if he is grasped and held by a superior power."

The intense inner self of Wojtyla has not, though, detracted from his outer self, as perhaps one might expect, but rather has been an inspiration to his humanity and emboldened his love. There is, at least in part, in his compelling need for the companionship of his fellow man his stated regard of Christ in every human being. And clearly this in turn has helped Wojtyla in his writing and speaking to fashion a concept of democracy of participation and moral principles.

His regard for Christ is also the pulse of his passionate pleadings for global human rights, his human warmth, and his compassion for the afflicted. Alongside this is Wojtyla's affinity with nature, and his prolonged participation in its pleasures: skiing, hiking, swimming, canoeing. To describe Wojtyla with that delightful Polish phrase, "a man for dancing and the Rosary," is not enough. The natural and supernatural are merged in his mind and heart, with a power greater than in most previous popes, resulting in a determination to serve both man's spiritual and secular needs.

3. Poland's Democracy

The third of these Polish parts was a democracy at which the West marvelled but from which it took no example or lesson for itself. Yet, might we not consider that Solidarity in its membership, and in its nationwide communal interlocution, and efficacy, was a more real democracy than that of most of the free world's countries—and thus an example for the whole world? While Western man has retreated into the shell of dominant executives, the Poles in sixteen glorious months returned democracy to its proper and magnanimous proportions: the demonstrative will of the people was made the accord of government.

As much a democracy of true popular participation, it was one of Christian ethics, which have as a particular point of reference regard for one's neighbor, unlike Western economies in which materialistic values are paramount. A particular Christian had become renowned in his land by more than twenty years of eloquent elucidation of the essences of ethical behavior. Now this man was Pope and carrying his caring message to a world audience. Poles still understood him best, however. In October 1979, just ten months before the Polish freedom strikes had erupted at the Gdansk shipyard, John Paul had stood before the General Assembly of the United Nations in New York and poured out the being of him and his manner of man:

> I would recall a constant rule of the history of humanity with regard to integral development and human rights. The rule is based on the relationship between spiritual values and material or economic values. In this relationship, it is the spiritual values that are pre-eminent, both on account of the nature of these values and also for reasons concerning the good of man. The pre-eminence of the values of the spirit defines the proper sense of earthly material goods and the way to use them.
>
> Man lives at the same time both in the world of material values and in that of spiritual values. For the individual being and hoping man, his needs, freedoms and relationships with others never concern one sphere of values alone, but belong to both.
>
> In reality, what justifies the existence of any political activity is service to man. In the final analysis this activity comes from man, is exercised by man, and is for man.

The foundations of those words were deep in the Polish people. In example, as an outgrowth of his preaching and university lecturing on the principles of ethics, Father Wojtyla, in 1957, was asked by the editor of the widely read Catholic journal *Tygodnik Powszechny* to pen a series of twenty-one articles entitled "Ethics for Beginners." In the 1958 New Year edition of the journal, Wojtyla wrote that Christian ethics not only protected "the social virtues which are such a priceless legacy of the Revelation of Christ," but also protected "the very foundation of these virtues in man and their *raison d'etre* in the individual human being." A person, Wojtyla continued, "is a free human being, but this freedom does not mean a detachment from society. A person is a free being within the framework of social life. He makes good use of his freedom when he develops real social virtues on the natural basis of his inclinations to social life. These virtues at the same time determine the fulfillment of the common good. A human being cannot develop and improve without this common good."

By the 1980 birth of the independent trade union federation, Solidarity, whose membership became 9-1/2 million, the bulk of the nation's working people, Catholic Poland was well grounded in the moral principles Karol Wojtyla had helped lay out and lead for its guidance.

Karl Marx had written in 1875 that "the emancipation of Poland is one of the conditions for the emancipation of the working class of all Europe." Had a process, which was begun through Wojtyla's Slavic and East European communion, and of which providential Solidarity was only part, come to fruition in May 1981 when Wojtyla was to have been back in Warsaw—had it not been stopped by a bullet to his stomach—then Marx just might have been proved right, though in a way he would never have dreamed of.

Chapter 3

The Polish Parts Help Make Europe Whole

Wonderfully, Marx *was* to be proved right—and in a way he most certainly would never have dreamed of. Seven short years later, in 1989, the three Polish proportions helped make Europe whole. Poland, that most Catholic of countries, began the emancipation from Marxist atheism of that half of the European peoples who are mainly Slavs, and for whom there stood the first Slav pope. The deed would be done in just 30 months.

Another five short years, to October 1994, and the foreign ministers of democratic Poland, Hungary, Romania, Bulgaria, the Czech Republic, and Slovakia sat down in Luxembourg with their counterparts of the European Union (which grouped most of the western half of the continent's governments) to discuss closer union.

East and West Germany had been one nation for four years.

The Baltic states of Lithuania, Latvia, and Estonia, now with none but their own soldiers on their soil, were the orbit of the Scandinavian countries, and keen too for eventual membership in the European Union.

The mighty Ukraine, with its 53 million population, was

a European sovereign nation by its people's own persuasion.

Russia had its name upon maps again, with a democratically elected State Duma and President, and with no domain beyond its old borders.

The Polish Peter had said in February 1990, at a General Audience in St. Peter's Square: "Directly from the Jasna Gora sanctuary, the voice of the Mother of God repeats with new strength, 'Believe the Gospel.' This she says to us Poles, to our neighbors, those who are our closest kindred, to all of Europe...'Believe the Gospel.'"

Four months later, in June, he told another General Audience: "In 1966, the Church in Poland, together with the entire country, thanked the Blessed Trinity for the gift of Baptism, which had occurred a thousand years before. In 1988, the thanksgiving for the gift of Baptism involved Christians in all of the nations which trace the origin of their Christian faith and their history to Kiev: Russia, Ukraine, Byelorussia (Belarus). A thousand years earlier, Vladimir, Duke of the Rus, did what the Polish Duke Mieszko had done a little while before." Poland was walking with history, and leading central and eastern Europe into a new destiny in God—and Wojtyla knew it.

The Pope had gone home to Poland for his third pastoral visit in June, 1987. As the week-long tour progressed, the Pontiff's language became more blunt. He asked pointedly if the structures of Poland's socialist state were "working against the common good." Solidarity was the touchstone of his social critique. "The people are on the threshold of frustration because of the economic and human rights situation," he said at Gdansk, whose shipyard industries were the birthplace of Solidarity. Before banner-waving and chanting crowds, John Paul spoke both *to* and *for* his people, confirming the Church's role as the protector of Poland's political opposition.

Rolling Solidarity strikes through 1988 forced Poland's Communist Party chief, and martial law enforcer, General Wojciech Jaruzelski to a round table agreement in April 1989, to allow some touches and strokes of democracy on the canvas of dictatorship. (When the Pope had arrived in Warsaw to begin his 1987 sojourn, Jaruzelski had tried to claim that "there is an emerging constructive co-existence between Church and State.") In parliamentary elections after the round table agreement, on June 4, 1989, all the seats in a new upper house were able to be contested democratically by any party, but this concession by the regime was only available to one-third of the seats in the lower house, the more powerful Sejm. All but one of the seats available to a universal suffrage vote were won by Solidarity.

The dam began to break. The impact of this overwhelming popular support brought forth in Poland in August a Solidarity-led parliamentary coalition under Prime Minister Tadeusz Mazowiecki, a stalwart of the 1980-81 movement.

The Pope, in a message to the Polish Episcopal Conference on September 1, 1989, to mark the 50th anniversary of the invasion of Poland (which began World War II and the stark division of Europe), concluded by quoting from the Book of Revelations: *"Behold, I make all things new"* (*Rev.* 21:5).

On October 5, 1989, John Paul received in audience Poland's Ambassador to the Holy See, Mr. Jerzy Kuberski, and said: "I share with the whole nation the joy for what is new, great, and much desired. I place the entire promising future, through the intercession of the Queen of Peace, in the hands of the almighty and merciful God.

"Today Poland is once again the country of courage and of events which have prophetic impact, above all for those parts of the world where human beings are still suffering, where particular social groups, or groups which confess the same religion suffer, where there is no general agreement regarding that good which is the human person himself, his dignity and the things produced by him so that he can be in the image and likeness of God."

On November 9, 1989, the Berlin Wall fell. Ukraine declared independence on July 16, 1990. The Communist flag of the hammer and sickle was lowered from the Kremlin masthead at midnight, Christmas 1991.

And how peacefully these Soviet-modeled, east European regimes had been put aside, falling like dominoes, and then the leviathan Soviet Union itself. These were subjugated peoples numbering in excess of 300 million, over whom were legions of secret police, huge armies, and vast conventional and nuclear armaments. And against men who had long stood in dictatorship: Poland's Jaruzelski, East Germany's Honecker, Bulgaria's Zhivkov, and Romania's Ceausescu. And Gorbachev, for all the *perestroika* of his personality, did not intend the break-up of the Soviet Union.

Surely, in Romania (which was not part of the Warsaw Pact) there were about 1200 deaths as the Army fought against Securitate secret police units in the overthrow of Ceausescu and his wife. But the overall passivity and peacefulness of the victory that this Pope—and let us mark it well—had sought was phenomenal.

"We give thanks to Our Lady of Jasna Gora for the gifts received, thanks for the gift of historic change, or rather the very numerous changes," the Pope told a General Audience in Rome on February 21, 1990.

"Everyone who witnessed last year's events which took place in Poland and in central and east Europe," he went on, "must give a confirmation that these changes happened. From a human point of view, one could have doubted their outcome. Still, they happened. And what's more, they happened in a bloodless fashion, with only one sad exception. A true 'peaceful revolution'—or rather an evolution propelled by an awareness of truth and proper freedom. Without the use of violence. Thus it was during the years of Solidarity: 1980-81. Thus it was in 1989."

From the West there had been a perception of the 1980s' Polish and east European history that was special. The leaders of the four main national props of Western democracy and Christianity, who had looked upon poor Poland in 1982—Britain's Margaret Thatcher, West Germany's Helmut Kohl, France's Francois Mitterrand and America's George Bush, as Vice-President and then President—witnessed the events of 1989. What did this concentration bring forth in explanation of the events? Their comments were shallow and self congratulatory. The "Cold War" had been won by the West. The Warsaw Pact had not been able to withstand the arms race with the West, they said.

The hand of the living God was unseen by these Western leaders. The valor and vitality of the Poles in the trials and tribulations of their difficult decade was unappreciated. A plenary place for the Polish and Slav Pope was unacknowledged.

So that we may understand this Pope, in order to understand what has been, and what is yet to come, we will now proceed upon his life. We will pursue the parts of this Pole and priest in whom social and spiritual values are fused in a possibly unique way.

Chapter 4

How Began His Manner of Man?

That ours is now a world lacking in high principle and compassionate purpose presses upon us a clear choice: we can either accept we are unable to influence the system of things, or act against the predominant values of our time. That it is easier to conclude the former than to commence the latter might be an immediate judgment, though not necessarily the more logical. For man is a social being and manifests himself in the company of man. He must by his actions, therefore, influence those around him.

Only we ourselves, after all, can be responsible for the alienation of human beings. It is a fallacy to claim that the "dehumanization" of our present-day civilization is caused by the system of things—the system of government, the system of production and distribution of material goods, the blind pursuit of progress, and so on. We create the systems of government, production, forms of technical civilization, utopias of future progress, programs of social organization of human life. The list could go on. Thus it is up to us to prevent any forms of civilization from dehumanizing and causing the alienation of the individual. It is the alienation of human beings from their fellow

21

men—for which all must be responsible—which is the main cause of any subsequent alienation from the system of things.

The previous paragraph has been taken, deliberately, as a paraphrase from page 297 of a momentous and innovative work of philosophy titled *The Acting Person* (D. Reidel, Holland). The author in his 300-page text moves man as an individual to heights and insights which may not have been secured before, then demonstrates that his transcendent nature can only be fulfilled within the community, in the performance of actions together with others. That comprehension of democracy—because of what is natural in us—electrifyingly takes one into a style and sense of "government by the people" so penetrating as to make one conclude that the author of *The Acting Person* is the outstanding living advocate of democracy:

"Participation is closely associated with both the community and the personalistic value. This is precisely why it cannot be manifested solely by membership in some community but through this membership must reach to the *humanness of every man*. Only because of the share in humanness itself does the dynamic feature of participation attain its personal depth as well as its universal dimension."

This secure and eager intellectualism can be gauged by his own statement in the book's preface, that the text is an attempt at reinterpreting certain formulations proper to the whole philosophy of the problem of the human being as a person. The author makes clear that in his presentation of this problem he has not followed traditional philosophy, "and by traditional philosophy we understand above all the heritage of Aristotle, and, among the Catholic schools of thought, of St. Thomas Aquinas." When we acknowledge the genius of the Greek Aristotle, who explained and espoused the natural reality of the world, and that St. Thomas Aquinas was the greatest mind of the second millennium of Christianity—the "Universal Doctor of the Church"—we have an early appreciation of the intellectual achievement of the author.

The Acting Person was first published in Polish, in 1969. It was revised and translated into English by Andrew

Potocki, with help from its author. By uncanny coincidence, of the type one is often confronted with in this man's life, the second half of the revised book was returned to the author for his final proofreading shortly before the second of the two conclaves in Rome in 1978, at which he was to be elected Pope.

Yes, the author of *The Acting Person* is Karol Wojtyla, Pope John Paul II.

But this is taking us past what is, first, Wojtyla's vaulting conception of man. "With what veneration the Apostle of Christ utters the word 'man'!" John Paul exclaimed on October 22, 1978, during his homily at the Mass which marked the formal beginning of his pastoral mission.

To those who criticize him for his strong opposition to abortion, homosexuality, and pornography, his supporters say there should be understanding of the richness of intellect at work here, the intense love for what is human, that to remain fully human we must remain natural. They say that John Paul sees humanity through the eyes of the Creator, that each man and woman is made in the image and likeness of God, and is defeated in that capacity by unnatural acts. The Pope's 1993 encyclical *Veritatis Splendor* (The Splendor of Truth) on moral issues had a simple ground: the insistence that it is possible to discern moral truth. "If morality is founded on truth, it serves the genuine development not only of the individual but the whole of society," he wrote.

The Pope in *Veritatis Splendor* praises the modern age for "its heightened sense of the dignity of the human person and of his or her uniqueness." However, he then warns against "exalt[ing] freedom to such an extent that it becomes an absolute," and thus conscience becomes a law unto itself, and the individual sets his or her own standards of what is good or evil.

The Pope locates human freedom within the bounds of natural law. Natural law is universal: as persons, we are subject to it. To perfect himself. . . "the person must do good and avoid evil, be concerned for the transmission and preservation of life, refine and develop the riches of the material world, cultivate social life, seek truth, practice good and contemplate beauty. . . . By submitting to the common law, our acts build up the true communion of persons...."

"We are speaking precisely of each man on this planet, this earth that the Creator gave to the first man, saying to the man and the woman: 'subdue it and have dominion,'" John Paul wrote in his first encyclical, *Redemptor Hominis* (The Redeemer of Man), in 1979. "Each man in all the unrepeatable reality of what he is and what he does, of his intellect and will, of his conscience and heart," he continued in the encyclical. "Man who in his reality has, because he is a 'person,' a history of his life that is his own and, most important, a history of his soul that is his own. Man who, in keeping with the openness of his spirit within and also with the many diverse needs of his body and his existence in time, writes this personal history of his through numerous bonds, contacts, situations, and social structures linking him with other men, beginning to do so from the first moment of his existence on earth, from the moment of his conception and birth. Man in the full truth of his existence, of his personal being...in the sphere of society and very diverse contexts, in the sphere of his own nation or people...and in the sphere of the whole of mankind...."

Wojtyla moves man with almost magical ease from each individual's uniqueness to his and her intrinsic place in the community at large. But before we completely undam this river of Pope John Paul's intellect and follow its current and course to the particular exaltation of all men, we should first and properly go to its source—for his philosophy is nothing less than a genesis by which we can return to the rights of our humanity.

Always strong in faith as a youngster, it was in the early dark years of the perverse German occupation of Cracow that Wojtyla fully entered in his mind and heart the land of luminous light of intense love for Christ. It was via the writings and biographies of two Sixteenth Century Spanish mystics, St. John of the Cross, and St. Teresa of Avila. (During his ten-day pastoral visit to Spain in November 1982, John Paul termed St. John of the Cross and St. Teresa of Avila "the spiritual teachers of my inner life.")

At the beginning of 1945, Wojtyla was able to enroll as

a student for the priesthood in the Theology Department of the re-opened Jagiellonian University. He became a leading scholar, thorough in analysis of a problem, clear in the delivery of his solution. Wojtyla's overall performance was assessed as *eminente.*

He was ordained a priest on All Saints Day, November 1, 1946, aged 26, by Archbishop Adam Sapieha. With the communists beginning to assert control over Poland, the Archbishop sent his brilliant new priest to Rome's Angelicum University for two years to continue his studies of moral theology and philosophy. There, still enthralled with St. John of the Cross, he wrote a doctoral thesis of *The Concept of Faith in the Writings of St. John of the Cross.* Wojtyla was given a *summa cum laude* for his thesis and became a Doctor of Divinity. He became much studied, too, of the philosophy of St. Thomas Aquinas, who placed his pen over the whole of theology and morals and interwove the philsophical heritage of the natural world of the great Greek scholars.

But as he continued in Italy, and as he traveled between studies to other countries (including France) of what was now Western Europe, Wojtyla's sensitive mind began to transform, began to open to the world about him. That world was not of traditional theology and popular Catholicism. Perhaps the transformation had started, in fact, back in Cracow, at the Solvay chemical works on the edge of the city. There, in 1940, the 20-year-old Pole had begun to labor in a quarry, in order to possess a German-issued work card, which gave Wojtyla some hope of avoiding deportation. A university scholar when the Germans invaded, now for the first time, he was engaged in prolonged manual work; for the first time he had the constant company of workers. He became earnestly close to his fellow-workers, to their hardships, humanity, and humor. "The physical work I did as a youngster was at least as important for me as my intellectual training," the new Pope was to say in January 1979.

He was back in Poland after his time in Rome, in the late 1940s. The intimacy of the confessional, his close friendships with many young people (of which reminiscences and photographs abound), and his many community involvements as a parish priest continued to expand his mind to the problems of everyday life. The communist dictatorial state's maintenance of its unwanted will upon the Polish people drew his mind more intently to questions regarding freedom and duty, responsibility for one's actions, and to the requisite that an individual's position and rights be in precedence to any external institution. The individual was his concentration, though always with the conjunction that man exists together with other men. This was paced with his deepening spirituality; sometimes much of his night was given up to prayer.

He pursued a reading of philosophical works in his spare time, his precise intellect reaching into the whole region of metaphysics (of universal being and truth). He could now, however, weigh advanced theory upon the scales of everyday life experience. A form and insight of man in action was beginning to mold in his mind, and it was taking him onto a mental path few philosophers had trod. And, importantly in understanding Wojtyla by his writings, he was naturally seeing this man through the capabilities, qualities, and endeavors of his own self: a catholic curiosity, ease and directness in his relations with others, faithfulness to friends, the confidence of conviction, optimism and joy in his faith, a relish for the pleasures of nature, and unafraid of emotion.

In 1951, the Church hierarchy in the See of Cracow released Wojtyla from his parish duties so that he could study philosophy full time under the auspices of the Theological Department of the Jagiellonian University. The young Polish priest, the clean Slavic lines of his rounded face enhanced by intelligent, responsive eyes, began in fact by translating the principal work of Max Scheler. This early Twentieth Century German philosopher had become an important prop in the thinking of Wojtyla, which had become centered in a maxim that personal experience was the supreme form of reality.

Scheler had been a pupil and disciple of Edmund Husserl, founder of the phenomenological school of philosophy, which stresses the unity of acts of human cognition (knowing and perceiving). Phenomenology was becoming the dominant philosophy in Western Europe as the second half of the Twentieth Century began, and Wojtyla's mind was as far removed as any mind could be from the Marxist philosophy of captive Eastern Europe. Yet, he would say at this time, according to Polish author Father Mieczyslaw Malinski, in his book *Pope John Paul II: The Life of My Friend Karol Wojtyla* (Burns and Oates): "Phenomenology seems to me a fine philosophical instrument, but no more than that. It lacks a general world view, a metaphysic if you like, and it would be worthwhile to create one." Wojtyla wanted to make a complete statement about man, and do it through his own philosophy. That was a prudent Catholic priest aged in his early 30s speaking, who now knew the intellectual capability he had.

Wojtyla, in another sense, came naturally to Scheler, for in an echo of St. John of the Cross, love was central to the German's philosophy. Scheler had knitted together a theory of ethics whereby ethical values (moral principles derived from the teachings in the Gospels) are realized through emotions and feelings, not by a rational process. His body of ethics were an ideal—a general description without detailed confrontation with specific moral problems and without such concepts as rules and duty. Wojtyla looked this squarely in the face and, notwithstanding other ways Scheler had helped his thinking, said it wouldn't work. This was the conclusion of a man now firmly standing in the realities of everyday life experience.

In 1953, Wojtyla made formal his negative judgment of Scheler with the thesis he had been working toward: *The Possibilities for Building a System of Christian Ethics on the Basis of Max Scheler.* The thesis gained him a doctorate, his second. This "habilitation" thesis was, in fact, the last presented in the University's Theology Department before the communist authorities closed down the department. When he was at last able to make his second return home to Poland, as Pope, he was conferred with an honorary doctorate by Jagiellonian University rector, Professor Jozef Gierowski on June 22, 1983. During his response, John Paul gave an insight of his time at the University, and expressed his indignation at that particular act of communist cessation: "During the Occupation, while at the same time working in a factory, I began studies in the clandestine Faculty of Theology of the Jagiellonian University. It was the autumn of 1942. Amid the terrible trials of the War, I gradually discovered within myself a vocation to the priesthood—and I entered on a new road. First, it passed through the stage of clandestinity, until January 1945 when I resumed the normal course of studies in this Faculty. As a student of the Major Seminary of Cracow in those first post-War years, I was able to take part in the life of the academic society of the University; for a certain period of time, I was even vice-president of the Students' Fraternal Aid of the University—'Bratniak.' After the completion of my studies and the research doctorate in the Faculty of Theology, I continued to keep in touch with the University. In November 1953, I was able to receive the qualification in the field of Moral Theology. That was the last qualification in the Faculty of Theology of the Jagiellonian University before the Faculty was excluded—after almost six centuries—from the University structure: the oldest *Alma Mater* in Poland. My *Alma Mater!"*

The same year, 1953, Wojtyla began to lecture at the Cracow Theological Seminary on social ethics. In 1956, his intellectual prowess, learning, and ability to communicate was for all of Poland to acknowledge, for he was offered and accepted the Chair of Ethics at Lublin University (the only Roman Catholic university in Eastern Europe). Wojtyla had become a Professor. Two years later Pope Pius XII appointed him, at the age of 38, Auxiliary Bishop of Cracow.

The papacy is God's partnership with man in the particular. What led a man to the position of Pope can therefore be sensed as Providential. That is why it is not sufficient to say of Wojtyla in his formative years that his mind was different from his contemporaries. The perspective must also be of place, perserverance, prayer, and Providence.

This, then, was the philosopher priest who sought a new, experiencing approach to the human being; and who in the early 1960s prepared to define it formally. But had Wojtyla written *The Acting Person* under a pseudonym, you would not know the author was a Catholic, let alone an Archbishop (indeed Cardinal, when the book was published in Poland). The number of times God is mentioned can be counted on one hand. That makes Wojtyla's accomplishment all the more arresting.

Chapter 5

His Product, Our Person

Aristotle and St. Thomas Aquinas, in their philosophies, placed themselves, so to speak, *before* the human act. The intellect moves the will. The will moves all the faculties toward their end. An action presupposes a person. This has been the standard approach in different fields of learning that have as their object man's actions, and is especially true in that field of learning which has as its aim the comprehensive study of moral goodness and evil.

Karol Wojtyla in his philosophy, places himself *after* the act. Through actions, a person discloses the reality of himself. Good and evil manifest themselves in actions, and by actions they become a part of man. Actions are the keystone in revealing and understanding the reality that a person is. A person faces himself through the experiences of his actions. While this may be a turnaround from the standard approach—while indeed what was a fundamental precept of philosophy may have been stood on its head—it is still an insight by Wojtyla that is fairly straightforward. But what is this "person" who faces himself through the experiences of his actions, and who is the subject of *The Acting Person?*

Wojtyla writes: "The vitality of the human body is of an essentially vegetative nature; the life of the body itself is vegetative. In fact, the vegetation of the human being

29

begins with conception and ends with death. Practically nothing of the vegetative dynamism of the human body is mirrored in consciousness, but is rather a sequence of purely instinctive reactions that follow the way of nature itself.''

Rather, "action *reveals* the person." In following that short sentence from the paragraph on his exposition of our human body's vegetation, we have the first understanding that Wojtyla's explanation of man is of the transcendence of the person, and an incipient appreciation of the exalted plane the Polish writer is about to lift man to. "Action gives us the best insight into the inherent essence of the person. We experience man as a person, and we are convinced of it because he performs actions," Wojtyla says.

Wojtyla proceeds in his objective of understanding the human person. He says it is for the benefit of us human beings who risk becoming too ordinary even for ourselves. Wojtyla shows that we are unequivocally of the nature of morality (moral conduct). "Actions have a moral value: they are morally good or morally bad. Through an action that is either morally good or morally bad, man, as the person, himself becomes either morally good or morally bad." This, for Wojtyla, is "the proper moment of freedom," for it shows in man self-governance, a freedom identifiable with the experience of "I may but I need not." It is, he writes, "the structure of man's becoming, through his actions, morally good or bad, that freedom manifests itself most appropriately." This freedom to act—because man has possession of himself—marks the transcendance of the person over nature.

Being in the possession of himself, man can determine himself. The fact that man is his own judge means that the will—"every genuine 'I will'"—reveals, confirms, and realizes the self-possession appropriate solely to the person. Because of this self-determination every man actually governs himself, Wojtyla says, "He actually exercises that specific power over himself which nobody else can exercise or execute."

Because of this self-determination, "an action reaches and penetrates into the subject, into the ego," and forms a person's ego in one way or another. Man therefore fulfills himself in the performances of actions.

Wojtyla is now able to tell the reader forthrightly the position he or she has arrived at: "The performing of an action, through the fulfillment it brings, is co-ordinate with self-determination. To fulfill oneself means to actualize, and in a way to bring to the proper fullness, that structure in man which is characteristic for him because of his personality and also because of his being somebody and not merely something; it is the structure of *self-government* and *self-possession*. This structure serves as the basis of morality, and it is owing to this structure that morality as a modality of conduct participates in the innerness of man and achieves a measure of durability in him. Being a person, man is 'somebody' and being somebody he may be either *good* or *bad*."

Because a person may be either good or bad, conscience becomes central to the person in Wojtyla's philosophy, and the Pole presents a personalistic significance of responsibility that exalts the individual: "For he is at once the one *who governs* and the *one who is governed by himself,* the one *who possesses* and the one *who is his own possession.* He is also *the one responsible* as well as the one *for whom* and *to whom* he is responsible."

The function of the conscience, Wojtyla says, consists in distinguishing the element of moral good in an action and in releasing and forming a sense of duty with respect to this good. This is man's surrender to truth. "As manifested in man's conscience, the capacity to surrender to truth shows how deeply the relation to truth is rooted in the potentiality of the personal being of man." This is what is sometimes called the "rational nature" of man.

This leads Karol Wojtyla to another fundamental pronouncement: A person only fulfills himself in actions which are morally good; he is unfulfilled in actions which are morally bad. He follows this with an important appendage: "The fact that in the performance of an action man also fulfills himself shows that the action serves the unity of the person, that it not only reflects but also actually establishes this unity."

Wojtyla himself poses the consequential question: How

to be good and not bad; how, through action, to become good and how not to become bad? The word "duty" is pivotal in the answer. "It is in the conscience that there is achieved the peculiar union of moral truthfulness and duty that manifests itself as the normative power of truth. The explanation of the normative power of truth is to be sought in its reference to the sense of duty." Duty, he says, expresses the individual's social obligation toward other people and toward the whole society to which he belongs.

"Inherent in all the obligations man has toward other people and which are the foundations for the codes of moral and legal norms is the presupposition that a duty is a specific interpersonal reality. It is a dynamic reality that forms an integral part of acting whereby the person—as we have more than once insisted—also finds the fulfillment of himself as a person." Truthfulness and duty are strictly concomitant.

Nor is this burdensome to man. Happiness is a natural result of this transcendant action. The state of happiness of the person comes "with the fulfillment of freedom through truth."

It is within these actions, too, that man's spirituality is provided and proved. "Our cognition of the spirituality of the human being comes from the transcendence of the person"—for by "spirituality" Wojtyla means an immaterial factor which is inherently irreducible to matter. Nor could man exhibit the spiritual element of his nature "had he not in some way been a spirit himself."

Wojtyla can now again address his exalted view of man: "The person can only partly and only in a certain respect be identified with nature, namely, only in his 'substantiality.' As a whole and in his intrinsic essence he reaches beyond nature. For the personal freedom repudiates the necessity peculiar to nature."

In this, Wojtyla has also found man's soul: "The 'experience of the soul' consists of what is attributed to the person's transcendence in action, namely obligation, responsibility, truthfulness, self-determination, and consciousness. We may add that the soul-body relation is also intuitively given—in an implicit way—in the experience of man as a real being. In this respect the subordination of the system of integration of the human person to the tran-scendance of the person in the action is revelatory.''

The Acting Person is a difficult and at times even a daunting book, a "severe philosophical volume," is how Lord Longford, in his biography, *Pope John Paul II* (Michael Joseph/Rainbird), describes the work, and for that reason writers who have made Wojtyla's papacy a subject have tendered short, cursory comments about the book.[1] This has been a detraction to our understanding man and the vitality and richness of Pope John Paul's mind. For there is in *The Acting Person* a complete statement about the human being by a magnificent mind. Man has been lifted onto a plane of capacity and capability which has simply not existed before as a written insight. As Wojtyla, prudent as he is productive, says himself in the book's preface, his is "a new approach to the human being," which he undertakes "in our own way."

There is the sovereign dignity of every person, which Wojtyla uniquely apprehends and applauds so wonder-fully, and the human rights that are all our due: "If we are to speak of the nature of the person, we can do so only in terms expressing the need to act freely."

Community

Having made his comprehensive statement about the human person, about the conjuction of freedom and truth, Wojtyla then proceeds to put that person into the commu-nity, into the "diverse communal or social relations in which, in most cases, human actions are involved." Com-munity means "acting and existing together with others."

Acting together with others, Wojtyla writes, corresponds to the person's transcendance and integration in the action. Thus "when man chooses what is chosen by others or even *because* it is chosen by others, he then identifies the object of his choice with a value that he sees as in one way or another homogenous and his own. This is connected with self-determination, for self-determination in the case of act-ing 'together with others' contains and expresses participa-tion." In line with this principle, then, on one hand everyone ought to strive for that kind of participation

---

1. Longford in his biography covers *The Acting Person* in half a page.

which would allow him, in acting together with others, to realize the personalistic value of his own action. On the other hand, any community of acting, or any human co-operation, should be conducted so as to allow the person remaining within its orbit to realize himself through participation.

"It is not only human nature that forces man to exist and to act together with others, but his existing and acting together with other human beings enables him to achieve his development, that is, the intrinsic development of the person. That is why every human being must have the right to act, which means 'freedom in the action,' so that the person can fulfill himself in performing the action."

This right can, though, be limited or definitely thwarted, Wojtyla says. This may happen in two ways: by "objective totalism" or by "individualism." He characterizes the dominant trait of totalism as the need to find protection from the individual, who is seen as the chief enemy of society and of the common good. (Wojtyla identifies the common good as corresponding to the social nature of man, which allows the person acting together with other persons to perform authentic actions and to fulfill himself and herself through these actions.)

The good advocated by totalism "can never correspond to the wishes of the individual, to the good he is capable of choosing independently and freely according to the principles of participation; it is always a good that is incompatible with and a limitation upon the individual. Consequently, the realization of the common good frequently presupposes the use of coercion." Totalism "unconditionally subordinates the individual to the community or the society." This was confirmed by "numerous historical examples," Wojtyla writes. He does not elaborate, but the words issue forth from the pen of a man who had been subjugated by a fascist invader and who now lived under a totalitarian communist regime.

Wojtyla's delineation of "individualism" as the second way man's right to freedom in action can be limited or thwarted may surprise, for—while again, not overtly stated—it concerns, perhaps primarily, us in the West in our materialistic consumer societies. And this expands our intimation in Chapter Two that Wojtyla's democracy has more properties, and is more profound, than democracy as presented in Western guise.

"Individualism sees in the individual the supreme and fundamental good, to which all interests of the community or the society have to be subordinated. Individualism limits participation, since it isolates the person from others by conceiving him solely as an individual who concentrates on himself and his own good. This latter is also regarded in isolation from the good of others and of the community. The good of the individual is then treated as if it were opposed or in contradiction to other individuals and their good. From the individualistic point of view an essentially constituent human property that allows a person to fulfill himself in acting 'together with others' simply does not exist."

He says: "We should note that in the thinking about man characteristic of these two tendencies, totalism and individualism, there seems to be no sufficient foundation for any authentic human community."

What, then, is an authentic human community? An authentic human community allows the actualization not only of participation but also of the fulfillment of the human being through the personalistic value of his and her action. That authenticity is kept by the attitudes of "solidarity" and of "opposition," Wojtyla writes. The one attitude cannot be dissociated from the other, he counsels.

Solidarity, that peculiarly Polish noun, means "a constant readiness to accept and realize one's share in the community because of one's membership within that particular community." Solidarity evinces regard for the "benefit of the whole," an awareness of the common good that makes a man "look beyond his own share." Solidarity means respect for all parts that are the share of every member of the community. But because the reference to the common good must always remain alive, there will be times when, of necessity, an individual will have to "take over more than one's usual share in acting and responsibility."

The attitude of "opposition" is not inconsistent with solidarity, he says. "The one who voices his opposition to the general or particular rules or regulations of the community does not thereby reject his membership; he does not withdraw his readiness to act and to work for the common good. This opposition aims then at more adequate understanding and, to an even greater degree, the means employed to achieve the common good, especially from the point of view of the possibility of participation."

There have, he continues, been innumerably different types of opposition in the course of man's existing and acting "together with others," in which persons "seek their own place and a constructive role within the community; they seek for *that* participation and *that* attitude to the common good which would allow them a better, a fuller, a more effective share of the communal life."

This leads Wojtyla to passionately counsel man to commit himself and herself to freedom of speech. "The principle of dialogue allows us to select and bring to light what in controversial situations is right and true, and helps to eliminate any partial, preconceived or subjective views and trends."

What is right and true always favors the development of the person and enriches the community, he says. "Dialogue, in fact, without evading the strains, the conflicts, or the strife manifest in the life of various human communities takes up what is right and true in these differences, what may become a source of good for men." Wojtyla knows that freedom to speak one's mind does not always make for plain sailing. Nonetheless: "...it seems that in a constructive communal life the principle of dialogue has to be adopted regardless of the obstacles and difficulties that it may bring with it along the way."

And now, through the word 'neighbor,' Wojtyla's great love of the person reaches its most sublime state as he takes his reader into the concluding pages of his book. "This brings us to the axiological moment of great significance. The notion of 'neighbor' forces us not only to recognize but also to appreciate what in man is independent of his membership in any community whatever; it forces us to observe and appreciate in him something that is far more abolute. The notion of 'neighbor' is strictly related to man as such and to the value itself of the person regardless of any of his relations to one or another community or to a society at large.

"The notion takes into account man's humanness alone, that humanness which is concretized in every man just as it is in myself. It unites human beings, all human beings who are members in different human communities. The notion of 'neighbor' refers then to the broadest, commonly shared reality of the human being and also to the broadest foundations of interhuman community. Indeed, it is the community of men, of all men, the community formed by their very humanness that is the basis of all other communities. Any community detached from this fundamental community must unavoidably lose its specifically human character."

Thus a person is capable not only of acting together with others; he is also capable of "participating in the very humanness of others. The ability to share in the humanness itself of every man is the very core of all participation and the condition of the personalistic value of all acting and existing 'together with others.' That is what is ultimately contained in the notion of 'neighbor.' "

The simple yet most splendid demonstration of egalitarianism—with the word "neighbor"—is made, it should be stressed, not by a Pope to befit the universality of his office, but by a Polish Archbishop who reached his understanding of man over the dictates of the regime which ruled his land.

Wojtyla then intensifies the concept of neighbor. The evangelical commandment, *'Thou shalt love,'* is invoked, which "entails the juxtaposition of my neighbor with my own ego: *'thy neighbor as thyself.'* " The commandment of love, Wojtyla writes, is also the measure of the tasks and demands that have to be faced by all men—all persons and all communities—if the whole good contained in the acting and being 'together with others' is to become a reality. In the two facts that everybody is a member of a community and everybody is a neighbor, there is contained every man's special relation to himself as a person and to his own ego. It follows that "we must remember in actual-life conduct the necessity of so co-ordinating acting and being 'together with others' as to protect the fundamental and privileged position of the 'neighbor.' "

Suddenly, where Karol Wojtyla's journey of man has

taken him is abundantly clear: in order to afford us the best protection from the dangers of alienation, our concern must be to make the system of reference to our neighbor the ultimate criterion in the development of the co-existence and co-operation of people in the communities and the societies that are established at different levels and according to different intracommunal bonds.

Any human community which allows this system of reference to become defective, Wojtyla warns, "condemns itself to becoming unfavorable for participation, and throws open an unbridgeable gulf between the person and the community. It leads to the disintegration of the community itself."

There, in its magnificence and munificence, is Karol Wojtyla's stimulation and summation of man and the interrelation of all men in humanness. His book is the product of an original mind which sought the practicality of man—the experience of the person—and found it in the transcendence of truth in action, an uplifting which can show us we are more than what we may believe we are, and a vital neighbor to each other, all in a secular profile.

But is there a practical example of his conception of man for us to follow, to recover from the obvious alienation of our years, and to achieve the democracy and dignity that Wojtyla insists is our right by the very fact of our being?

Chapter 6

We Are All Solidarity

The term "God given" is not one always well met in this day and age. The phrase "uncanny coincidence" (which we have used already in this book of episodes in Karol Wojtyla's life) is, though, hardly an adequate characterization of what occurred in the first two years of John Paul II's papacy to construct a revelatory and remarkable passage to his manner of man. By arrangements begun several years before the two papal conclaves of 1978, in 1979 *The Acting Person* was published in English, the language that links more nations in understanding than any other tongue.

The next year, the latter part of the book metaphorically became the stuff of world headlines as the solidarity Wojtyla had so persuasively advocated and argued for came to be. Solidarity became a dynamic national but pacific movement of democracy which held its presence of popular participation against formidable foes for sixteen months.

"The attitude of solidarity is, so to speak, the natural consequence of the fact that human beings live and act together; it is the attitude of a community, in which the common good properly conditions and initiates participation, and participation in turn properly serves the common good, fosters it, and furthers its realization... In accepting the attitude of solidarity, man does what he is supposed to do not only because of his membership in the group, but because he has the 'benefit of the whole' in view: he does it for the 'common good.'" It is there on pages 284-285, and under a subheading "The Attitude of Solidarity."

Had Solidarity impacted itself sooner on Poland, during the time of Pope Paul VI, Cardinal Wojtyla would have been acknowledged as an embryonic and emphatic voice in the movement's vocation. Wojtyla had, indeed, begun placing his principles of participation in Polish minds before even the election of Pope Paul's predecessor, Pope John XXIII, which was in 1958, as we have seen in example in Chapter Two. His ideas and ideals of democracy had their literary denouement in the 1969 Polish-language publication of *The Acting Person*. Upon that, his intellect had become publicly the most potent in Poland. There was joined to that his strong moral position of Cardinal and Deputy Primate in this country of a large Roman Catholic majority.

Nor was his an abstract intellectualism: all theory and no action. He was a man of concrete endeavor who had confronted the communist authorities numerous times in pursuit of religious freedom and freedom of speech. A famous example of this, and a great monument to his perserverance, is the large, modernistic (its roof the shape of a huge open ark, its sculptures inside stark and perspicuous) Church of St. Mary at Nowa Huta, a steelworks town four miles from Cracow. The town was founded in the early 1950s, and by command of the Marxist regime was to be without a church. Wojtyla and the workers by their will overcame that fiat eventually. Building began in October 1967. Almost ten years later, on May 15, 1977, Cardinal Wojtyla consecrated the completed church. During his sermon on that day he said: "Nowa Huta was built as a city without God, but the will of God and the people who work here has prevailed. Let this be a lesson."

When Solidarity came in the mode and mold Wojtyla had advocated, his advice belonged now to much more than Poland. By the universality of his office, Wojtyla's words were now for the world.

The Pope himself showed his sense of this in his encyclical *Laborem Exercens* (On Human Work), which he published in September 1981 (when Solidarity was still the dynamic physical force of the common good in Poland). "In order to achieve social justice in various parts of the world, in the various countries, and in the relationships between them," John Paul wrote, "there is a need for ever new movements of solidarity of the workers[1] and with the workers." Meeting delegations of workers at Czestochowa on June 18, 1983, during his second papal return home, John Paul told them the deeds of Solidarity had touched hearts and consciences around the world.

The bright light of Solidarity's determined life burnt in an East European darkness cast over by the huge Soviet neighbor perversely determined in anti-Christian domination. Communism had implanted and protected its own atheistic agency in Warsaw, but this only made greater the impact of Poland's free trade union federation upon the world's collective psyche. How quickly imperialist Soviet forces had in 1956 and 1968 snuffed out the prescriptions of the Hungarian and Czech peoples to be masters of their own lands. That the twelve-year gap between 1956 and 1968 was repeated between 1968 and 1980, the year Solidarity came into being, without Moscow swiftly acting to stop the Polish popular movement is made the more astounding by the fact that just before, in December 1979, Soviet forces had, without compunction, invaded their Asian neighbor, Afghanistan.

Yet despite our appreciative attention, we had no sense of a universality in Solidarity. In Poland in 1980-81, though, the system of things was changed emphatically for the better by popular, peaceful participation. The system of things in the West is demonstrably failing us in some fundamental aspects. Then why in our supposedly democratic states have we been unable to do as the Poles, in their much more difficult and dangerous circumstances, did and make the necessary changes for the better?

Perhaps it is an important enlightenment that Wojtyla, in his advocations of democracy, gives only small reference

---

1. In the encyclical, the Pope describes work as "any activity by men and women, whether manual or intellectual, whatever its nature or circumstances."

to the holding of national elections. There is in Wojtyla's writings an echo of Pericles, whom we might call the original exemplifier of democracy, and who orated in Athens that: "Although only a few may originate a policy, we are all able to judge it. We do not look upon discussion as a stumbling block in the way of political action, but as an indispensable preliminary to it."

Wojtyla in *The Acting Person* adds another indispensable, on pages 286-287: "In order for the opposition to be constructive, the structure, and beyond it the system of communities of a given society, must be such as to allow the opposition that emerges from the soil of solidarity not only to *express* itself within the framework of the given community but also to *operate* for its benefit. The structure of a human community is correct only if it admits not just the presence of a justified opposition, but also that practical effectiveness of opposition required by the common good and the right of participation." How many executives in the West give grace and place to ideas for the betterment of the common good that originate from people whom those executives deem to be political opposition?

The Pope is a great admirer of the Swiss type of "direct democracy." During a visit to that country in June, 1984, John Paul even spoke of the "political genius of Switzerland"—whereby, through nationwide referendums on important social and economic questions, the will of the people is constituted the work of their government. Wojtyla brings it all back to the word "participation." Participation, he shows, is what is natural and necessary in the individual man and woman. When the means of outward participation are denied, the inner person (the self) is retarded.

Participation in its broadest sense means involvement in the national decision making process. To the individual, participation (the human action) is probably the most fundamental manifestation of the worth of the person himself and herself. Thus, as we said in Chapter Four, Wojtyla has drawn to men and women democracy's greatness and goodness through the natural capacity and compulsion of each human being.

What may be even more striking when we look back a

shorter span of history, only to 1989, is to see that, when Solidarity's success became permanent, against the sort of odds that we have already recounted, it led not just Poland but half a continent out of the darkness of alien values. And when we come forward the few years to our present days, we in the West have a fairly general complaint that we are not at all well served by our parliamentarians. Yet how do we in the West like to see the events of 1989-91? We like to say that in the West versus East match up, the West won. Is there something of a contradiction here?

The English-speaking world has boasted a dedication to parliamentary democracy. Why, now, is there so much popular distaste for governing politicians? Recent electoral matters have been extraordinary. The October 1993 Canadian general election saw the ruling Progressive Conservatives, who held 157 seats in the 295-seat Ottawa parliament, reduced to a mere two seats, neither of which were the Prime Minister's, Kim Campbell.

The November 1994 mid-term American elections saw ruling Democrat incumbents removed in droves, so that the party lost its majority in both arms of Congress, the Senate and the House. Many state governships fell out of the Democrats' hands to the opposition Republicans.

Opinions polls in Britain, early in 1995, showed support for the ruling Conservative Party at around 22 percent, while that of the main opposition party, Labour, had a support level of about 56 percent—the biggest gap in 50 years.

In the author's own country, New Zealand, there have been violent swings in popularity the past decade between the two main parties, National and Labour, culminating in a 1993 national referendum decision to introduce a new voting system that should represent more political parties in Wellington's parliament in the hope of forcing a more consensus regime.

Dissatisfaction with the people we have been electing to govern us appears deep (hence the catchcry "Kick the bums out"), which presumably would not be so if they were doing what we wished. For our will to be the government's way—for society to be what we want to live in for our common good—it would seem we must be directly responsible for the laws and regulations which govern us. If Solidarity was at times something of a rough and ready movement, its sophistication of function is to be found in Switzerland. It may be that this type of government is beginning to appear in America through the propositions on some states' ballots. If so, we remind ourselves of the needs of minorities, and the poor and weak, which, again, is about the Gospel values of Solidarity.

To suggest that we confer with a Pope about our secular political contretemps may be one of the more original propositions. Yet, Wojtyla does state an attractive thesis: governments should be our function, rather than we be governments' function.

Chapter 7

The Worker

In his poem, "The Quarry," which Father Karol Wojtyla published in a Polish Catholic journal in 1957, there is a simple yet sublime line which enthuses, again, his great regard for the worker:

"Hands are the heart's landscape."

Wojtyla's esteem for the worker is very much part of his intellectualism and humanitarianism, part of his experience. His background is proletarian. Karol's father, before early retirement due to ill-health, had been an army officer on the regional draft board; before her marriage, his mother was a school teacher. To his enthronement as Archbishop of Cracow early in 1964 (he had been Acting Archbishop since 1962), Wojtyla invited workers of the Solvay factory where he had labored during the Occupation.

"Through work man must earn his daily bread and contribute to the continual advance of science and technology and, above all, to elevating unceasingly the cultural and moral level of the society within which he lives in community with those who belong to the same family." The words begin John Paul's encyclical, *On Human Work*.

"Work is one of the characteristics that distinguish man from the rest of creatures, whose activity for sustaining

45

their lives cannot be called work," the Pope goes on in the encyclical. "Only man is capable of work, and only man works, at the same time by work occupying his existence on earth. Thus work bears a particular mark of man and of humanity, the mark of a person operating within a community of persons."

Often, the word "worker" carries a precursory reference to the color of a collar, blue or white. Not with Wojtyla. As we quoted him earlier in this book from this encyclical: "Work means any activity by man, whether manual or intellectual, whatever its nature or circumstances."

Toil is something that is universally known, for it is universally experienced, he says in the encyclical. It is familiar to those doing physical work under sometimes exceptionally laborious conditions, familiar to agricultural workers, to those who work in mines and quarries, to steelworkers, to those who work in builders' yards and in construction work. It is likewise familiar to those at an intellectual workbench; to scientists; to those who bear the burden of grave responsibility for decisions that will have vast impact on society. It is familiar to doctors and nurses. It is familiar to women, who, sometimes without proper recognition on the part of society and even of their own families, bear the daily burden and responsibility for their homes and the upbringing of their children.

Work thus embraces all humanity and is at the center of our being. John Paul describes work as "an activity beginning in the human subject and directed toward an external object." This leads him to counsel again the dual manner of participation, within and without: "The process of work embraces all human beings, every generation, every phase of economic and cultural development, and at the same time it is a process that takes place within each human being, in each conscious human subject." Through work, man "not only transforms nature, adapting it to his own needs, but he achieves fulfillment as a human being and indeed, in a sense, becomes 'more a human being.'" It also makes natural his assertion of the priority of labor over capital. "Work is for man and not man for work." When one looks at the effect of unemployment on the many millions of people out of work in the Western world, the sense of his words strike home with force. "No to the scandal of unemployment which deprives workers of their major right, the right of all to earn their daily bread by work!" the Pope cried during a visit to Brussels, Belgium, in May 1985.

Capital is defined by him as "the whole collection of means of production," a description that is a general embrace of economic systems. "Everything contained in the concept of capital in the strict sense is only a collection of things," he says. "Man," however, "as the subject of work, and independently of the work that he does—man alone is a person." He goes on: "This truth has important and decisive consequences." He would overturn with his pen the economic systems—and they exist in the West as in the East and the Third World—which make man an object of materialism, and remake man subject of his social situations.

John Paul is prepared to confront the 19th and 20th Centuries of industrial and economic history with the exclamation: "Labor was separated from capital and set in opposition to it, and capital was set in opposition to labor, as though they were two impersonal forces, two production factors juxtaposed in the same 'economistic' perspective. This way of stating the issue contained a fundamental error of economism, that of considering human labor solely according to its economic purpose." He told several thousand workers gathered in Rome on December 9, 1978: "I know how necessary it is that work should never be a thing to alienate and frustrate, but should match the higher spiritual dignity of man."

Practical illumination of what Pope John Paul was to write in his encyclical had been given by him in March 1981, during a visit to the Terni steelworks in Italy. "It is the workers who are the principal cause of production," he said, "and because they are human persons, they are not an instrument to be used by others. Other things are instruments, but they are not, for they are men, and they are the primary and substantial cause of what they produce. And so they have the right to the fruits of their labor. That means not only a fair wage, but a certain sharing in the management of the firm, and a share in the profits."

"I know the needs of the working class, their just demands and their lawful aspirations," John Paul said in his December 1978 address to workers in Rome, part of which we quoted above.

Nor did he apologize for the fact that it was a papal pen which delivered the words of his document. "I know what it means to work in a factory for all those hours of the day, every day of the week, all the weeks of the year," he told factory workers in Milan in May 1983. "I learned this on my own body. I did not learn it from books."

Nor was he deferential to the ruling regime—as another visiting statesman would probably have been—if working conditions of part of the populace of the country he was in were not what they should be. In the Philippines in February 1981, he spoke sharply in defense of the Filipino rural poor: "It is not admissible that people who work the land must continue to live in a situation that offers them no hope for a better future. Land is a gift of God for the benefit of all. It is not admissible to use this gift in such a manner that the benefit it produces serves only a limited number of people, while the others—the vast majority—are excluded from the benefits the land yields. In such situations the Church will not hesitate to take up the cause of the poor and to become the voice of those who are not listened to when they speak up, not to demand charity but to ask for justice." Indeed in February 1986, the Roman Catholic Church in the Philippines played an important role in the overthrow of the Marcos dictatorship.

Typically John Paul concludes his encyclical *On Human Work* by drawing the reader back to Christ. "The truth that by means of work man participates in the activity of God Himself, his Creator, was given particular prominence by Jesus Christ—the Jesus at whom many of His first listeners in Nazareth *were astonished, saying, where did this man get all this? What is the wisdom given to him?... Is not this the carpenter?'*"

John Paul goes on: "Jesus not only proclaimed but first and foremost fulfilled by His deeds the Gospel, the word of eternal wisdom, that was entrusted to Him. Therefore this was also 'the gospel of work,' because He who proclaimed it was Himself a man of work, a craftsman like

Joseph of Nazareth. And if we do not find in His words a special command to work—but rather on one occasion a prohibition against too much anxiety about work and life—at the same time the eloquence of the life of Christ is unequivocal: He belongs to the 'working world,' He has appreciation and respect for human work."

Ten years later, on May 15, 1991, 100 years to the day after Pope Leo XIII's great social critique *Rerum Novarum*, John Paul II returned to the subject in relish with another encyclical, *Centesimus Annus*, to mark that centennial. He looked with satisfaction at how the world was changing, the liberation of many workers from situations of injustice and oppression, a world more in keeping with the vision of Pope Leo.

John Paul heads the third chapter in his encyclical simply "The Year 1989." His homeland and central parts of Eastern Europe were free of Marxist socialism. He notes also the fall from power of authoritarian regimes in the Third World, especially Latin America (Brazil, Argentina, and Paraguay are obvious examples). This is important to the Pope for it is estimated that by early in the third millennium the Americas will represent half the Church's membership.

John Paul condemns "new forms of religious fundamentalism" which deny some sectors of the community their right to exercise their civil and religious rights—in the Middle East and on the Indian sub-continent perhaps most obviously. (The Pontiff has deplored the tragic civil war in the Sudan, where the Muslim north from the capital Khartoum has been trying to force the Christian south to convert to Islam. Rwanda, in 1994, caused him great anguish—a considerable majority of that country's peoples are Christian.)

As the new world order evolved, and democracy became more the norm, John Paul in his new encyclical endorsed the concept of the market economy—but carefully. "It would appear that, on the level of individual nations and of international relations, the free market is the most efficient instrument for utilizing resources and effectively responding to needs." However, very much in keeping with the thrust of *On Human Work*, he insists that "the purpose of a business is not simply to make a profit, but to be a community of people at the service of society." Further on he puts it another way: "The Church acknowledges the legitimate role of profit, but other human and moral factors are at least equally important." Therefore, "capitalism is to be rejected if it lacks an ethical and religious core."

He writes of capitalism: "**Yes**, insofar as capitalism is an economic system which recognizes the fundamental and positive role of business, the market, private property and the resulting responsibility for the means of production, as well as free human creativity in the economic sector. **No**, if by capitalism is meant a system in which freedom in the economic sector is not circumscribed within a strong juridical framework which places it at the service of human freedom in its totality and which sees it as a particular aspect of that freedom, the core of which is ethical and religious."

The new encyclical recognized that land and capital, once decisive factors in production, are being replaced in importance by the abilities of people themselves. "Today technology, knowledge, and skill are more important in modern economic systems than land or capital. Initiative and entrepreneurial ability are becoming increasingly decisive." But many people "have no possibility of acquiring the basic knowledge which would enable them to express their creativity and develop their potential. This is very much the case with the poor."

During his many foreign tours of Latin America and Africa, John Paul has persistently taken the side of the poor and the oppressed. The Pope, though, is against the "liberation theology" that had gained some ground in Latin America by the 1980s, a theology which sought to build 'Christian teaching around Marxist ideas like class struggle. A careful Vatican document on "liberation theology," issued in April 1986, emphasized that the Church's essential mission, following that of Christ's act of sacrifice to redeem humanity from sin, "is a mission of evangelization and salvation." The document goes on: "In this mission the Church teaches the way which man must follow in this world in order to enter the kingdom of God. Her teaching, therefore, extends to the whole moral order, and notably to the justice which must regulate human relations."

The social message of the Gospel, therefore, John Paul writes in *Centesimus Annus,* "must not be considered a theory but above all else a basis and a motivation for action. The Church promotes those aspects of human behavior which favors a true culture of peace, as opposed to models in which the individual is lost in the crowd, in which the role of his initiative and freedom is neglected."

John Paul addresses environmental concerns. "Ecological well-being cannot be safeguarded simply by market forces. State intervention is necessary." Humanity stands first and foremost in the globe's resources, of course. Thus, "in addition to the irrational destruction of the natural environment, we must also mention the more serious destruction of the human environment. Too little effort is made to safeguard the moral conditions for an authentic human ecology."

"In a certain sense," John Paul goes on, "the guiding principle of Pope Leo's encyclical, and of all the Church's social doctrine, is a correct view of the human person and his unique value as made in the image and likeness of God, and as having a transcendent destiny."

The dignity of the worker, and the dignity of work was the hallmark of Pope Leo's encyclical, the Catholic Church's great social charter as the world was industrializing. Among the rights of the person, he said in 1891, were the rights to private property, the right to establish professional associations of employers and workers, or of workers alone (trade unions), the right to rest, the humane treatment of women and children, and the right to a just wage. He insisted on necessary limits to the state's intervention, as "the individual, the family, and society are prior to the state."

Pope John Paul takes satisfaction that the Church's teaching on social and human rights was an initiating role "in the great upheavals which took place in Poland in the name of solidarity." He sees the economic problems for Poland and its neighbors that followed their overthrow of Marxist socialism. "The radical re-ordering of economic systems, hitherto collectivized, entails problems and sacrifices comparable to those which the countries of Western Europe had to face in order to re-build after the Second World War.''

He asserts the Western world's monetary obligation to Eastern Europe, but, with remarkable charity, the Slav Pope says, ''This should not be at the expense of the Third World which has even greater needs.''

Chapter 8

Of Morals and Mass Destruction Weapons

In his appointment before God, and in the application of his own deep human compassion, John Paul II has stressed two concerns during his papacy: man's alienation and dehumanization, and the menace from the many weapons of nuclear warfare. The two concerns naturally coalesce in his mind. Man's lack of regard for the rights and dignity of his fellow man—our poor moral behavior—is most potently manifest in our weapons of mass destruction. Reconciliation in our human race is available through Jesus Christ "who is God and who is love," the Pope asserts.

There is a widely held belief that nuclear warheads and atomic bombs, these awesome weapons of destruction, are somehow apart from our human nature. John Paul's perception, however, is that man's mind is the maker of humanity's systems, and that man's moral judgments command what he has constituted. This is why the parallel, in the past two decades, between the rise in the production of nuclear weapons, and the decline in man's moral behavior and the "break" in Western man's mind from God, comes upon the Pope with force and fear.

One part of man's immorality, weapons of mass destruction, cannot be divorced from his and her other immoralities, the Pope believes. He wrote in *The Acting Person* that an individual achieves self-fulfillment through actions which are morally good, while an allegiance to bad moral values leads to non-fulfillment. Now that we possess "the terrible mechanism of general destruction" is the proportion of our failure to be fulfilled.

"Surely the time has come for our society to realize that the future of humanity depends, as never before, on our collective moral choices," the Pope said in February 1981 at Hiroshima. He continued: "Our future on this planet, exposed as it is to nuclear annihilation, depends upon one single factor: humanity must make a moral about-face."

"It is man who kills and not his sword—or, in our day, his missiles," John Paul said on Christmas Day 1983 in a special message commemorating the Roman Catholic Church's 17th World Peace Day.

Pope Wojtyla's passionate humanitarianism comes forth most profoundly when he speaks against nuclear weapons, while his strictures on morals bring him mostly criticism, with complaints of "conservatism" and even "sternness." In his encyclical letter *Dives in Misericordia* (On the Mercy of God), which he published in December 1980, John Paul wrote that: "One cannot fail to be worried by the decline of many fundamental values which constitute an unquestionable good not only for Christian morality but simply for human morality, for moral culture. These values include respect for human life from the moment of conception, respect for marriage in its indissoluble unity, and respect for the stability of the family. Moral permissiveness strikes especially at this most sensitive sphere of life and society. Hand in hand with this go the crisis of truth in human relationships, lack of responsibility for what one says, the purely utilitarian relationship between individual and individual, the loss of a sense of the authentic common good and the ease with which this good is alienated."

John Paul went on: "If any of our contemporaries do not share the faith and hope which leads me to implore God's mercy for humanity in this hour of history, let him at least try to understand the reason for my concern. It is dictated by love for man, for all that is human, and which, according to the intuitions of many of our contemporaries, is threatened by an immense danger."

Nuclear weapons are no longer an East-West question. And the man who fundamentally understands this has, uniquely in the history of the papacy, come out of the East to the West to embrace the world. He posed the question at Hiroshima: "Will this weapon, perfected and multiplied beyond measure, be used tomorrow, and if so would it not probably destroy the human family, its members, and all the achievement of civilization?"

The way back from this threat to a human existence is manifestly by the path of a recommitment to and rejuvenation of good moral values, which are the stuff of dignity and decency, the Pope says.

And does this not bring home to us again how important (not just for Poland) Solidarity was, with its pivot of Christian ethics? Christ's plan for society was that it live as one family in justice, truth, freedom, and love, the Pope said in a special 1984 New Year Day message of peace. "This family will only be united in deep peace if we hear the call to return to the Father, to be reconciled with God Himself," he continued.

Ten years later the Vatican designated 1994 as "The Year of the Family." Leading a two-day celebration of the family in Rome in October of that year, John Paul encouraged families from around the world to "draw strength from the faith and resist the 'social decay' of contemporary culture." But he was distressed in a speech at the end of the year to Italian clergy, referring to "truly terrifying facts" which had come to light on the fate of children in certain countries. He denounced "the brutal massacre of street children, the prostitution into which they are forced, and the trade practiced by organizations selling body parts for transplant."

On Sunday, Christmas Day 1994, he told 40,000 people gathered in St. Peter's Square that war was continuing to create many innocent victims. He referred to what he called the interminable war going on in Bosnia, and stressed the dangers of more recent conflicts in the Russian Caucasus and in Africa.

The Church's opposition to nuclear war and abortion are part of its strong pro-life stance. The Church looks with particular irony on the fact that some people both oppose nuclear arms and support abortion—without insight of their contradiction. At Nowy Targ, Poland, in June 1979, the new Pope said: "If the right of man to live is transgressed at the very moment when he starts to become a human being, in his mother's womb, then the entire moral order—which indirectly serves to protect the inalienable welfare of man—is jeopardized."

Women were intimately connected to the mystery of life, John Paul also said in the 1984 New Year Day message of peace we quoted above. "They could therefore do much to advance the spirit of peace, in their care to ensure the preservation of life, and in their conviction that real love is the only power that can make the world livable for everyone."

Nor is it the office of pope which has brought John Paul to his conclusion of the correlation of atomic armaments and man's alienation. "Man must discover himself, must completely rebuild himself, must completely redeem himself," Cardinal Wojtyla pleaded during a sermon in Cracow in May 1978. "Man is an image of his God—God made him unto His own likeness. Man redeems and discovers himself when he steps into this image; when he discovers his own likeness to God."

So, too, did the threat to all humanity from nuclear bombs impel itself upon him during his episcopal years. Several weeks after the election of Pope John Paul I, and before the Pope's sudden death, Cardinal Wojtyla spoke in Mogila, Poland, of the "unimaginable danger of a new war which is always with us and in our minds."

His fears for man drove harder upon him when he became responsible for man in the especial position Christ Himself created. His plea for comprehension at large of why man must return to God and remake a moral covenant with Him became so urgent that he momentously and unexpectedly announced 1983 would be a Holy Year.[1] "May the Holy

---

1. There was drama in the very maneuver. The Catholic Church traditionally has a Holy Year once every twenty-five years. The last had been in 1975, dedicated to devotion to Our Lady on the 25th anniversary of Pope Pius XII in 1950 having made the Assumption of Our Lady (the belief that Mary's

Year be a sign and symbol of new access to Christ," he said in his November 1982 papal bull which proclaimed the Year. Its theme would be repentance and reconciliation, the Pope said.

In the homily of his Mass in St. Peter's Basilica on the March 25, 1983, Feast of the Annunciation, which officially began the Holy Year, the Pope made plain what had led him to his announcement. The world was headed for catastrophe, he said. "Protect the nations and the peoples," he prayed to God. "Do not permit the work of destruction that threatens humanity today!"

At his 1983 Easter Mass, a week after the Holy Year's commencement, John Paul was trenchant, calling on mankind to submit itself to Christ's power, then pronouncing: "The more you notice the hour of death on the horizon of your history, submit yourselves the more fully to His power." He had said during a homily at New York's Yankee Stadium, in October 1979: "In the midst of a world that is anxious about its own existence, Jesus does not merely give us peace. He gives us His peace accompanied by His justice. He is peace and justice. He becomes our peace and our justice. What does this mean? It means that Jesus Christ, the Son of God made man, the perfect man, perfects, restores, and manifests in Himself the unsurpassable dignity that God wishes to give to man from the beginning."

And in the depths of American alienation, Harlem, during that same 1979 tour, John Paul spoke perhaps the most beautiful line of his papacy. He told of the joy of knowing Christ, then came the line—"For we are an Easter people and 'alleluia' is our song."

The Pope has even compared modern industrial man to the Gospel's prodigal son, during a visit to Austria in September 1983. "The prodigal son in his unbridled quest for freedom is, it seems to me, the image of man in the society

---

body was taken into Heaven at the end of her life) a dogma of Catholic faith. Thus the next Holy Year had not been due till the start of the third millennium, the year 2000. John Paul said the 1983 Holy Year would celebrate the 1950th anniversary of the Redemption of mankind by the Passion, Death and Resurrection of Jesus Christ.

of the highly developed nations," he said in Vienna. "Rapid technological and economic progress and rising standards of living have led many to believe that God has become expendable. But this self-confident exodus, this rejection of God, is soon followed by great disillusionment coupled with fear."

There were two paramount poles of materialism in the world today: the communism of the Union of Soviet Socialist Republics, and the consumerism of the United States of America. These two countries have engaged in the biggest manufacture and deployment of nuclear devastation weapons.

It may have been a more prophetic than opinionated statement when Cardinal Corrado Ursi of Naples, as he was about to enter the Sistine Chapel for the October 1978 conclave, had said: "It will be in the reign of the new Pope that we shall see the decisive battle between materialism and Christian humanism. The Holy Father will have much to suffer." Just two years and seven months after Cardinal Ursi's declaration, Pope John Paul lay in a Rome hospital bed, severely wounded by pistol shots after an attempt to murder him directed by that nation most intent on the destruction of Christian ideals and their replacement by materialistic values.

As John Paul looked back from the 17th year of his pontificate to the pronouncements of the early years of his reign, he could esteem a world now seemingly made safer from the threat of nuclear war. No question, the United States and the four sovereign republics of the former USSR on whose territory there had been stationed strategic (long range) nuclear weapons—Russia, Ukraine, Kazakhstan, and Belarus—had made large strides in the reduction of nuclear arsenals.

In December 1987 had come the first treaty to abolish an entire class of nuclear weapons. The United States and the USSR agreed to the elimination of the two sides' ground-launched ballistic and cruise missiles with ranges of between 500 km and 5,500 km.

The START I accord had been signed between the two sides in July 1991; unilateral cuts in tactical and strategic nuclear arms by both sides had followed a few months later.

Immediately after the political collapse of the USSR, Russia's President, Boris Yeltsin, had offered further cuts and proposals, as had US President, George Bush; agreement was made for the transfer to Russia of all Soviet tactical nuclear weapons stationed outside Russia; written commitments were entered into by Ukraine, Kazakhstan, and Belarus to give up strategic nuclear weapons stationed on their territory; and the START II accord was signed in January 1993.

If all these agreements and unilateral initiatives are fully implemented, Washington and Moscow will have reduced their strategic and tactical nuclear arsenals from a combined total of almost 47,000 weapons to some 13,500 weapons, a reduction of more than 70 percent. There were also efforts to take tactical nuclear weapons away from operational commands and move them to central storage, to take a large number of strategic forces off alert, and to take intercontinental ballistic missiles "off aim."

While all the good things were happening about nuclear weapons' reductions by the two super-powers, in the last year of his presidency, Mr. George Bush would still warn, in a July 13, 1992, statement, of his country's concern that regional nuclear powers were not making similar efforts.

India and Pakistan, whose relationship has frequently been tense, are both known to have a small nuclear arsenal and missile means to deliver the bombs. China, which in 1993 was estimated to have between 250 and 400 strategic and tactical nuclear weapons, continues to build up its arsenal, and was reported at the end of 1994 to be building two new types of ballistic missiles. In 1994, Israel had up to 200 nuclear weapons, according to Britain's authoritative *Jane's Intelligence Review,* twice that of a decade ago. Iran and Iraq also want the bomb; North Korea's military, too.

A regional nuclear conflict on the Indian subcontinent between India and Pakistan, or a conflict between India and China, might bring. . .350 million deaths, a tragically high number. But that figure, 350 million, is also an estimate of the number of abortions—babies killed in the womb by their mothers—during the pontificate of John Paul II.

The abortion figure is not exaggerated to shock, and in actuality may be larger. Moscow admitted in 1988 that the yearly rate of abortions in the Soviet Union was 9 million. The annual rate for Western countries combined is certainly into seven figures, as we would presume for China, where the regime seeks to enforce a stricture of one child per family.

May there now be understanding of why this matter moves the Pope so powerfully? It does not concern the Pope how strong may be the forces aligned against him on this most basic of moral issues, he will stand firm. As John Paul directly stated in March 1993, during a general audience in St. Peter's Square: "The Roman Pontiff must speak the truth. Woe to him if he were to be frightened by criticisms and misunderstandings." The Pope's task, he went on, was "to do now and always what Christ asked Peter to do when the two met after the resurrection on the shore of the Sea of Galilee: *'Feed my lambs.'*"

Mother Teresa of Calcutta is simple and direct in her truths. She told students of the Oxford Union, England, in 1993, during an address about abortion: "We must not destroy what God has created so beautifully."

"Woe to you if you do not succeed in defending life," John Paul cried out later in the year, at the World Youth Day Mass in Denver, Colorado, attended by close to half a million. "Cherish life in Christ," he pleaded, "and share that life with others."

Some of the most trenchant criticism of the Church was heard during the September 1994 United Nations population conference in Cairo, as Vatican delegates strove, with the help of some Catholic and Muslim countries' diplomats, to eliminate from the conference's final declaration all reference to abortion as a means of holding the world's population to 7.8 billion by 2050, from today's 5.6 billion. Many of the Western countries' delegates, including the head of the American delegation, Vice President Al Gore, were hostile to the Vatican pressure. But the Pope's men were successful. Into the Cairo declaration went an explicit statement that "in no case" should abortion be promoted as a method of family planning.

Heaven's eye appears sharply on America in this issue. In October 1992, with the Bosnian civil war at its worse, a small group of American Catholics made a hazardous journey down the Dalmatian coast and inland to a village called Medjugorje, the holy place where Our Lady appears daily in apparition to several visionaries. Naturally satisfied with the achievement of their arrival, the American group was stunned at the sharp words to them by Vicka Ivankovic, one of the visionaries, on behalf of the Blessed Virgin Mary, about their country's level of abortions and poor morality. "They really got an earful," recalls a New Zealander at Medjugorje the same week. Another of the visionaries, Marija Pavlovic Lunetti, was to say later that the Gospa, as they call Our Lady in Croatian, "has spoken to us forcefully many times about abortion, saying 'Abortion is a great sin. I call upon you to help and to protect life.'"

Added significance concerning the American group at Medjugorje may have been in the timing, the eve of the Presidential election that would bring the Clintons to power. We recollect the televised words of Hillary Rodham Clinton soon after she became First Lady, that American law should be changed to allow abortion on demand.

As a prelude to the Cairo population conference, Mr. Clinton, following again in his wife's footsteps, had, in March 1994, issued a directive to American embassies abroad that "the United States believes access to safe, legal, and voluntary abortion is a fundamental right of all women." The Pope's reaction was to fear that "for the first time in the history of humanity, abortion is being proposed as a means of population control."

When John Paul was in Poland in June 1991, during his fourth pastoral pilgrimage to his homeland, he spoke of a "vast cemetery" in the world, "that of the unborn, of the defenseless whose faces even their mothers had not seen before allowing, or being pressured into allowing, that their lives should be taken away from them before their birth. They were alive, they had been conceived and were growing in their mothers' wombs, unaware of the mortal threat which was looming large. And when that threat had become a fact, those defenseless human beings tried to defend themselves."

He then became very personal, and very revealing: "A

film camera has recorded a desperate defense against aggression by an unborn child in its mother's womb. I once saw such a film and to this day I cannot free myself from what I saw. I cannot free myself."

Many Americans do seem to have come to the realization of the necessity to rejuvenate the morals of their society up out of the trough they have slumped to. The Pope has spoken to them: "It is within the everyday world that you must bear witness to God's kingdom. You are called by God Himself to work for the sanctification of the world from within, in the manner of leaven. In this way you can make Christ known to others, especially by the witness of your lives."

Chapter 9

But Not to the Holy Land

It was after all from the Holy Land, nineteen and a half
centuries ago, that his faith had come. The passion with
which the Pope spoke was understandable. "Oh! How I
wish I could go to the land of my Lord and Redeemer!"

They listened to him, the many gathered in St. Peter's
Square on that second Sunday in December 1978, less than
two months after his election. "How I wish I could find
myself in those very streets in which the people of God
used to walk at that time, to climb to the top of Sinai,
where the Ten Commandments were given to us! How I
wish I could pass along all the roads between Jerusalem,
Bethlehem, and the Sea of Galilee! How I wish I could stop
on the Mount of the Transfiguration."

These were natural sentiments for a Vicar of Christ to
hold, and Wojtyla's sensitivity and great love for the Son
of God would have inflamed his wish to walk where Jesus
and His Mother had made the mind of the Polish Peter.
Indeed, he continued: "This was and is my greatest desire,
ever since the beginning of my pontificate."

The many assembled before him waited in expectation
of John Paul's announcement of the date on which he
would travel to Israel. He himself reminded them all of the
"immense joy of the bishops gathered in the second session of the Second Vatican Council on hearing the words

of Pope Paul VI who, in the address delivered at the close of that session, had announced to them that he would go—for the first time—as a pilgrim to the Holy Land.'' Paul VI's journey to Israel, in January 1964, was undertaken less than a year after his papacy had begun.

Having built the St. Peter's Square crowd's expectations to the heights, John Paul let them drop with a thud. ''But, though regretfully, I must, at least for the present, forgo this pilgrimage, this particular act of faith, the significance of which can be more deeply understood by the Bishop of Rome, who is the successor of Peter. In fact, Peter comes just from there; it was from the land of Christ and Mary that he came to Rome.''

''At least for the present?'' More than 16 years later the situation had not changed. In the meantime, John Paul had become far and away the most traveled pope in the history of the Church, had gone 200 times into foreign countries (some of which he has visited more than once). What is it that has stopped him from going to the Galilee of the Gospels, where Jesus worked His many miracles to prove His divinity, to the Jerusalem of the Last Supper where Jesus made His body and blood of bread and wine, and left to those who seek Him that supreme gift of Himself in the Eucharist by the power of the Holy Spirit in the priest's consecration?

He has not said what directly; that is not usually his way in a matter in which he has made a great personal sacrifice. From certain public statements of his, however, we can express our certainty of the reason why this most traveled of St. Peter's successors has not gone to the great and holy place of Peter. During his speech to the United Nations General Assembly in October 1979, John Paul expressed a fervent hope that a solution to the Middle East crisis might draw nearer. He was prepared to recognize the value of any concrete step or attempt made to settle the conflict, but went on: ''I want to recall that it would have no value if it did not truly represent the 'first stone' of a general over-all peace in the area, a peace that, being necessarily based on equitable recognition of the rights of all, cannot fail to include the consideration and just settlement of the Palestinian question.''

(Israel occupied the 2200 square mile West Bank and the smaller Gaza Strip—which are home to 1.4 million Palestinians—during the 1967 Six Day War. Israel acted in violation of international law which forbids a military occupier [which Israel became] from changing domestic law and administration [which Israel did]. The establishment, within 15 years of occupation, of more than 100 Jewish settlements for 35,000 Jews in the territories—which the Israeli government liked to call by their Biblical Hebrew names, Judea and Samaria—seemed, almost, the de facto annexation of the territories by Israel. Nearly all the West Bank's urban Palestinian areas were surrounded by Jewish settlements and isolated from one another to shatter the geographic continuity of Palestinian land.)

The Six Day War, when the old city of Jerusalem, that most holy and significant of places, came back to Israel after 2000 years, would have made a considerable impact on Wojtyla's mind. A week before the War's commencement, Pope Paul VI announced that he was to make the Archbishop of Cracow a cardinal. Two weeks after the War's conclusion, Wojtyla formally received his red hat from the Pope at a consistory in Rome.

Pope John Paul became most outspoken in defense of the Palestinian people when Israel invaded Lebanon in June 1982. After the first news reports of the invasion reached the Vatican, the Pope actually expressed his wish to go to Beirut, capital of Lebanon, according to Vatican sources quoted by Reuter News Agency, but was dissuaded by Curia officials because of the security risk. Israeli guns were drawn around the western half of Beirut, in which was trapped 10,000 members of the Palestine Liberation Organization. Israelis began firing fearful barrages on to the civilian areas of that part of the city, while John Paul publicly condemned the "brute force" of Israeli armor, and appealed again for recognition of "the rights of the Palestinian people."

He sent Mother Teresa of Calcutta (winner of the 1979 Nobel Peace Prize), for whom he has great admiration, to West Beirut, to demonstrate solidarity with the victims of the Israeli bombardments. There, on August 15, Mother Teresa rescued 37 handicapped children from a badly shelled hospital which had flown Red Cross flags since June.

The next month the Pope met the PLO leader, Yasir Arafat, in the Vatican. During that Vatican audience with Arafat, John Paul spoke against "recourse to arms and violence in any form and above all to terrorism and reprisals." The Pope called for a Middle East peace that recognized "the right of the Palestinians to a country of their own."

This is what John Paul's sacrifice is about—and it is a fair measure of the man. He would not go to the land of his heart's great impulse until the West Bank and Gaza Strip Palestinian people lived there in their own homeland, that the conduct of their affairs was in their hands. And we can gauge the personal impact of this sacrifice by such papal comments as that on November 18, 1990, given to crowds in St. Peter's Square before he prayed the Angelus: "My thoughts go to the Holy Land, so dear to every Christian's heart."

The "Intifada"—the West Bank and Gaza Strip mass resistance to Israeli rule, begun in 1987 and evidenced most abundantly by stone throwing youths—only increased the enmity between Israel and the PLO. Israel's harsh response did not stop at torture.

Two years previously, at the beginning of October 1985, Israeli F-15 fighter aircraft had swept in from a long, low flight over the Mediterranean to bomb the PLO headquarters at Hammam Ash-shatt near Tunis. Yasir Arafat's working quarters were destroyed, and 60 PLO men were killed. Unknown to the Israelis, Arafat was briefly away from his place on that day.

While the Pope well understood the deep frustrations of the Palestinian people in the years of the Intifada, he wanted the violence to end. "Let us ask the Lord to inspire in leaders a real will for peace so that, with the help of the international community, the Palestinian people and the Israeli people may obtain the justice and security they aspire to," John Paul said in 1990.

"For decades the Palestinian people have been treated unjustly!" he cried out in January 1991. "The Palestinian people are begging to be heard, although some groups have opted for unacceptable methods to make themselves heard."

What a change has taken place! That astonishing hand-shake on the White House lawn on September 13, 1993, an adjunct, too, of the gracious offices of the Norwegian government, brought forth self rule under PLO authority to the Gaza Strip and Jericho in the West Bank and an enclave around the city. Then came the 1994 announcement that the year's Nobel Peace Prize had been won jointly by...the PLO's Arafat and the Prime Minister of Israel, Yitzhak Rabin and his Foreign Minister, Shimon Peres.

Agreement by agreement, the West Bank was coming under Palestinian rule. That which the Pope had pleaded for, what he had made so great a personal sacrifice to, was coming to fruition. At Christmas, 1995, the Manger Square in Bethlehem should, for the first time in years, be free of swarms of Israeli soldiers toting assault rifles. If the world does not understand the Pope's sacrifice, perhaps Arafat has some insight. On Christmas Eve 1994, he extended a gracious invitation to the Pope to visit the Gaza Strip.

A wider nations peace, too, was settling upon the borders of Israel. When John Paul was elected to the papacy, only Egypt, of the Arab countries, was in consideration of formal acceptance of the state of Israel. Now there are hands of friendship reaching across the Jordan River, that hallowed place of Christ's public commencement, with Israel's Rabin and Jordan's King Hussein meeting in each others' capitals in 1994, after the signing of a formal peace treaty, and establishing embassies. Morocco and Tunisia have respectively opened a liaison bureau and interest section in Tel Aviv, and Kuwait said, late in 1994, that it too wanted to open an interest section there. Syria's leader, Hafez Assad, loser of the Golan Heights back in 1967, no longer spoke with belligerency against neighbor Israel, if reluctant to make concessions to advance the peace process.

A major Middle East economic conference at Casablanca, in November 1994, showed a wider acceptance of Israel—its Prime Minister, Rabin, attended by invitation (though the regimes of Iran, Libya, and Iraq stayed away). Israel's agricultural and industrial expertise and its superb techniques of water management would willingly be shared to help build economic strength amongst Middle East nations, Rabin said.

Pope John Paul had watched, appalled at the vast destruction of Lebanon by its civil war and Israel's invasion. "Faced by the repeated tragedies experienced by all who live in Lebanon, we have become increasingly aware of the extreme danger which is threatening the very existence of that country," he had said, in September 1989, in an apostolic letter to all the bishops of the Catholic Church on the situation in Lebanon. "Lebanon cannot be abandoned to isolation. I have not hesitated to knock at every door so that an end may be put to what must truly be called the massacre of an entire people," he went on. He pleaded many times for the release of Western hostages, relatives of whom he gave public comfort to.

"Lebanon has been in agony under the very eyes of the whole world for years," he told ambassadors to the Holy See, in January 1991, "yet there has been no concrete action to help the country free itself from elements and external forces exploiting it for their own ends."

Now Lebanon—"a land visited by Jesus"—is peaceful and generally unified, with a functioning parliament. Certainly, industrial and residential re-construction is moving at a fairly slow pace, and the country is under the strong influence of Syria (which has 30,000 troops there), and there are southern portions which are the place only of the Hizbollah Islamic terrorist militia confronting Israel. It is true, too, that the Pope, in 1994, wanted again to visit Beirut, and his aides had to tell him again that his safety could not be guaranteed there. Still, what a change from what was.

There is still a way to go before all the West Bank is under Palestinian statehood. The terrorist power there of "Hamas" and the smaller "Islamic Jihad," in religious and racial hatred opposed to the existence of Israel, and to which the PLO has been in bloody opposition, may not be easily overcome. There will be tension concerning the large Jewish settlements on the West Bank, and more so if there are attempts by right-wing Israelis, as there were early in 1995, to construct more such settlements there.

Then there is east Jerusalem, which the PLO wants as

the Palestinian capital, and which Israel says will remain eternally with the newer western half of the city, Israel's capital. "Jerusalem," the Pope said in 1993, "that city which is holy *par excellence* and dear to all three monotheistic religions."

For the Pope, he has now completed his sacrifice. In the streets of Jerusalem where Jesus made His great sacrifice, on the shores of Galilee, the Pope's reward awaits him.

Chapter 10

The Signs of
St. Maximilian Kolbe

If there is one 20th Century personality whom Pope John Paul especially admires, it is that of Maximilian Kolbe, a saint and fellow Pole.

The tide of emotion that the drama of the 1941 death in Auschwitz of Saint Maximilian, a Franciscan priest, evokes in the Pope is beyond easy comprehension. There were, after all, other singular acts of heroism in the World War II death camps, and several thousand Polish priests died by German hands. But Karol Wojtyla has gone so many times during his priesthood into Maximilian Kolbe's death cell, has espoused the man so greatly—"he is a patron for all of us in this difficult century"—one must ask what are the intimate well-springs at work in the Pontiff's mind that draw him to this saint?

The official texts of all speeches John Paul delivered during his June 1979 heartful visit to his homeland, together with an array of color photographs taken during those nine days of national communion and celebration, were assembled as a book, and published by Collins under the title *Return to Poland.* The book's publisher worked closely with the Vatican (there is an introduction by the editor of

L'Osservatore Romano, the Vatican's newspaper), and consequential regard might be taken of the book's front cover photograph. In poignant pathos, the Pope stands at the entrance of Father Kolbe's death cell, long red cape over his white cassock, rosary in hand, his lowered face strained in contemplation.

"It is well known that I have been here many times. So many times! And many times I have gone down to Maximilian Kolbe's death cell. Father Maximilian voluntarily offered himself for death in the hunger bunker for a brother, and so won a spiritual victory like that of Christ Himself. A victory through love and faith which overcame the world." So spoke John Paul at Auschwitz (or Oswiecim as he properly calls the place by its Polish name) during that visit.

Karol Wojtyla would have known of Maximilian Kolbe before 1939. Not just a Franciscan father, Kolbe, who had a wonderful mind and eyes very direct in their look, was the father of Poland's Catholic journals and newspapers. After the 1918 rebirth of Poland (the country had for almost one and a half centuries been partitioned between Russia, Germany, and Austria), Kolbe began in Cracow, at the age of 27, to publish the magazine *The Knight of Mary Immaculate.* It was 1922, after a year long battle in a sanatorium against tuberculosis. He was the magazine's founder, editor, director, dispatch clerk, and was determined to bring the message of joy and reconciliation in Christ to every Polish family. The title of the magazine showed Kolbe's deep devotion to Mary, and his belief that Christ could always be reached through His mother.

By 1927, Father Kolbe had somehow gotten together enough money to establish, with other Franciscan priests and laity, a town-monastery called Niepokalanow (City of the Immaculate), thirty miles from Warsaw, and to equip it with the latest printing machines. It became the foremost publishing center in Poland.

The Knight grew to a circulation of 750,000 copies. Seven specialized reviews were published, even a daily newspaper, *The Mary Dziennik,* with a circulation of 250,000.

In 1930, Father Kolbe established another Niepokalanow, in Japan, of all foreign places, on an incline fringing the city of Nagasaki. A Japanese version of *The Knight* grew to a circulation of 50,000. (When the atomic bomb was dropped on the city in 1945, *The Knight's* establishment was virtually unscathed.) A return of the tuberculosis brought Father Kolbe close to death in 1936, and his superiors in Poland called him home.

He was again director of his first Niepokalanow when Germany invaded. He and other Franciscans were arrested by the invaders, transported to Amlitz in Germany, and then three months later, on December 8, Feast of the Immaculate Conception, was unexpectedly returned to Niepokalanow. The Germans apparently, and quite stupidly, thought Maximilian Kolbe might collaborate with them.

Father Kolbe met his country's occupiers' invitation to recommence *The Knight* with a "trial issue" by defiantly writing in that issue: "No one in the world can change truth. What we can and should do is to seek truth and serve it when we have found it. There are two irreconcilable enemies in the depth of every soul: good and evil, sin and love. And of what use are the victories on the battlefield if we are defeated in our innermost selves?" The Gestapo came for him.

The gates of heinous and hideous Auschwitz, "the Golgotha of our times," John Paul has called it, closed behind Father Maximilian on May 28, 1941. His identity became number 16670.

Deemed capable of rigorous manual work—extermination was the alternative—he was put to work with others in a small farm field within the camp, tearing down trees and pulling off their branches, bundling them together and transporting them, all by bare hand. A month later, half-starved, Father Maximilian fell under the weight of a tree trunk he was carrying. Unable to rise, he was lashed fifty times by guards as he lay across the trunk, the imagery of Christ vivid in how and what he suffered.

Father Maximilian was left to die in a pool of his blood. Somehow, with strength from some place, he managed late in the night to drag himself back to his bunk block. Even in his delirium, as he lay on a paillasse, he could not curse his captors. "Hatred builds nothing. It is love which serves," he murmured several days later. To his pitiful fellow inmates he gave the constant encouragement of comfort in Christ.

A month later it was harvest time. Prisoners, including Father Maximilian, were working in the fields of Auschwitz. An escape was reported from that area of the camp. Ten prisoners would die as retaliation, the camp commandant shouted at the inmates assembled from the fields. He counted down. The tenth, a Pole named Franciszek Gajowniczek, staggered and cried out for mercy: "I have a wife and children...."

Father Maximilian stepped forward. He begged: "Take me. He has a family. I am alone. I am a Catholic priest." He added: "After all, I am old." He was 47.

Even the S.S. guards shook their heads at Father Maximilian's offer of his life in exchange for Gajowniczek's. God (and the camp commandant) accepted the sacrifice.

The prisoners were not allowed to speak to each other, but Gajowniczek and Father Maximilian exchanged glances. "I'll never forget the look he gave me as he was led off to die," Gajowniczek, who was to survive the war, has said.

The ten condemned were entombed in darkness and without food or water in the underground "hunger bunker." Father Maximilian would not let any of the other nine despair. He gathered them round him, and together at intervals they sang Polish hymns and prayed. After two weeks he and three others were still alive. Exasperated, the camp commandant ordered the four to be injected with deadly carbolic acid. Father Maximilian died in prayer on August 14, 1941, the vigil of the Feast of the Assumption.

Pope John Paul has spoken of the awe Maximilian Kolbe's courage provokes. But clearly, the Franciscan's sacrifice evokes a lot more than that in his fellow Pole. There seems to be something very personal here, something from the war years.

That crisis in young Wojtyla's life came on August 6, 1944, a Sunday. The people of Warsaw had suddenly risen up against the German occupiers of their capital, and in Cracow the Germans moved swiftly in a brutal *tapanka* ("pacification") to make sure the same did not happen

there. Men on the streets were seized. Some were shot, the
rest herded to the railway station for deportation. The
Cracovians' situation worsened when the Germans began
actually entering homes and dragging men out and into
patrol wagons, coloring the day's name in Cracow's history
"Black Sunday."

From his residence, 10 Tyniecka Street, where he had
a small, one room flat, Karol Wojtyla heard the sounds of
vehicles and of shots, then watched German troops and
Gestapo turn portentously onto Tyniecka Street.

At the outbreak of World War II, Wojtyla had been 19
years old. Until this August *tapanka,* he had survived five
years of severe occupation. He had been at risk, and knew
the risks. He had helped hide Jewish people around
Cracow, and disguise their identity. He had been part of
the underground university which defied the German edict
that all Polish higher education cease; been an actor in the
clandestine Rhapsody Theatre. Karol had entered Cracow's
esteemed Jagiellonian University in 1938, with excellent
high school grades, to study the Polish language and its
use, with a career as a classical actor his ultimate ambition;
and in 1942 he had begun to study theology in secret,
preparing to enter the priesthood. Any of these actions, if
discovered by the Germans, would have meant the death
penalty for the young Pole. And the Gestapo must have had
their suspicions about the peripatetic and cerebral Wojtyla.

Drenched by the deadliness around him—a quarter of
Poland's population perished during the War—as much by
the self-danger of his surreptitious anti-Nazi activities,
Wojtyla must have doubted his ultimate survival. All the
members of his immediate family were deceased, making
him even more sensitive to his situation.

Now he watched the Germans moving from the top end
of Tyniecka Street toward his residence, entering houses
and forcing men out at gun-point.

Wojtyla returned to his room, closed the door, but by
deliberate act did not lock it. He then lay face down on
the floor, arms outstretched, making the body the shape of
a cross—a Polish traditional submission to God—and
prayed.

This much we know. What particularly Wojtyla's prayers

were we do not know, and he would be about the last person to reveal them in the circumstances of his entreaties.

Wojtyla has spoken once about his priesthood vocation: to a poor family whom he visited as a young priest in the St. Florian parish of Cracow. While crossing Tyniecka Street in 1941, Wojtyla told the family, he was knocked down by a tram. When he regained consciousness in the hospital and came out of delirium, he felt a sudden strong call to the priesthood. Though deeply religious from an early age, he fended the call off, determined, when and how he could, to continue his university studies in Polish philology (a love of language he shared with Maximilian Kolbe), and pursue his acting ambitions—he was already highly regarded in Polish drama. Then a few months later, Wojtyla met with another serious accident, knocked down in another street by a truck. In the hospital again, and again he felt a strong summons to the priesthood.

Now, having met that call, death was close on Black Sunday, for the Germans had entered 10 Tyniecka Street. Only God's will stood between the intruding enemy and Wojtyla.

The Germans did not pass through that door. When Wojtyla was consecrated a bishop in 1958, he wrote upon his seal the Latin words *Totus Tuus*—All Yours.

God (and the Germans) allowed life to Wojtyla, while God (and the Germans) accepted the life of Father Maximilian. That, surely, is fused in Pope John Paul's mind.

The day after Black Sunday, Cracow's handful of students for the priesthood, including Wojtyla, made their way stealthily to the episcopal Bishops' Palace, summoned there by the Archbishop of Cracow, Adam Sapieha, where he hid them for some months till the Russians advancing from the east drove the Germans out of the city. Karol Wojtyla has referred often to Father Maximilian's declaration of himself in Auschwitz when he offered his life: "I am a Catholic priest."

The first meeting of Maximilian Kolbe's knights, as he called the group of young priests whom he banded together and from whom all his great publishing and spiritual enterprises were to ensue, took place in 1917 on the evening of October 16. In 1978 it was on the evening of October

16 that Karol Wojtyla was elected Pope. Father Maximilian was beatified (made Blessed) on October 17, 1971. Seven years later, the 17th of October was the first full day of Wojtyla's papacy.

It is also a remarkable fact that the two weeks of severe abdominal pain the Polish Pope shared with the Polish Primate, Cardinal Wyszynski, in 1981—the Pope had been shot through the abdomen; the Cardinal Primate was dying of stomach cancer—ended for the Primate on the fortieth anniversary of Father Maximilian's incarceration at Auschwitz, May 28. The Pope's continued pain, discomfort, relapse, sudden return to the hospital, and second operation (to reverse a colostomy), coincided exactly with Father Maximilian's time in Auschwitz. The saint died on the vigil of the Feast of the Assumption, while on the Feast itself, August 15, the Pope left Gemelli Hospital to commence what was, in time, a complete recovery.

It was Pope John Paul himself who raised Blessed Maximilian Kolbe "to the honors of the altar," formerly declaring his sainthood. This was on October 10, 1982, in St. Peter's Square in a spectacular canonization ceremony attended by a huge crowd, which included 81-year-old Franciszek Gajowniczek, the man for whom the saint gave his life, twenty-six cardinals, three hundred bishops, and 8,000 deeply moved Poles. "Greater love has no man than this, that he lay down his life for his friend," the Pope said, repeating the words of Jesus in St. John's Gospel. "St. Maximilian defended an innocent man's right to life...similar to Christ who gave His life on the Cross."

Two days before the canonization, the Polish ruler, General Wojciech Jaruzelski, and his communist henchmen in Warsaw, with a perverse sense of timing, had passed a law abolishing Solidarity as an independent trade union federation. (Martial law had been imposed on the nation the previous December.) At the ceremony, John Paul rounded on them: "The stifling of the legal and rightful activities of Solidarity is a violation of the fundamental rights of man and society. I ask all men of good will throughout the world to pray for the Polish nation."

The next day, the Pope stood before an official government delegation from Warsaw. Emboldened perhaps by the spirit of the new saint, he was even sterner, tongue-lashing the regime for its continued incarceration of several hundred Solidarity members. "Solidarity's gains cannot be lost," he added sharply.

A month later, a series of startling events proceeded. The regime announced that the Pope could make a return pastoral visit to his homeland the following June. That which was his by the right of his birth, that which was his heart's great desire, that which had been taken from him by autocratic, arrogant men, had been returned to him. Solidarity leader Lech Walesa was freed from internment, and then, two days before Christmas, many of the other imprisoned Solidarity members were released.

One might indeed wonder what power was at work in the aftermath of St. Maximilian's canonization. One wonders if there was within it a reflection of the humility of Pope John Paul II, who can so reverently esteem the deeds of his fellow Pole, yet speak no public word of any personal act of bravery or faith during the War years.

When he did return to Poland, in June 1983, the Pope traveled to Niepokalanow, and there, dressed in red vestments, at a huge outdoor Mass, presented to the Polish people the first saint of the second thousand years of their Roman Catholicism, Maximilian Kolbe.

Chapter 11

The Man

"Call me Karol not Cardinal," he asked Polish community members of Wellington amongst whom he spent some days in 1973. The New Zealand capital is as far a distance as civilization is from Cracow. Yet, even in that extreme, his manner was always of the compliment of friendship.

Five years and thousands of miles from that meeting, when he stood upon the floodlit central balcony of St. Peter's Basilica on the evening of October 16, 1978, the vast crowd before him in the Square had barely recovered from the shock of the Cardinal Deacon's announcement of a foreign pope, the first non-Italian for 455 years. They waited for his blessing, *Urbi et Orbi,* to the Church and the world, traditionally the only public words the new Pope spoke at this time. But now there was a second shock for the crowd when the Polish Pope indicated he would address them before giving the customary blessing. An incredulous Curia official standing next to the non-Italian Peter actually tried to stop him. "I will speak to the people," Wojtyla said quietly and firmly to the official.

His extempore address "in your—no, our—language" both sought and offered strength. In his exalted position, as in Poland, as in Wellington, wherever, there has been this vivid wish of Wojtyla to reach out with an unaffected hand and touch.

In 1973, in a private dining room in the Polish community of Wellington, the generosity and geniality of a rich
human personality came forth, as he refused to place himself above those gathered around him, as he listened and
laughed, as he sat there in a plain black cassock and told
anyone who addressed him as Cardinal that, actually, his
name was Karol. They marvelled that this was a prince of
the Church, one of the one hundred or so cardinals from
whom, amongst the hundreds of millions of their fellow
Catholics, the next pope would be chosen. Several of them
had difficulty restraining their surprise. Wojtyla saw this.
He went quiet. For a few seconds his eyes were down on
the carpet. Then he looked back up at them, and there, in
that room far from home, he explained: "So many of my
friends disappeared during the German occupation."

Those words are amongst the most revealing Pope John
Paul has ever spoken. He had seen how evil could impact
itself upon a whole nation, how few could be the years of
an individual life. He would live to a full capacity what
years were to be his—and he would live also for the friends
whose fullness never would be.

That is an attitude toward other people that cannot but
be generous in its regard and appreciation of them. Little
wonder the address from St. Peter's balcony, little wonder
his dislike of having deferential honor paid him, particularly of having his papal finger ring kissed, little wonder
that his first encyclical, *Redemptor Hominis,* should be
devoted entirely to the dignity of man and man's human
rights, little wonder his esteem for St. Maximilian Kolbe.

That the Cardinal, when in Wellington, should express
an affection for old people and ask to be able to visit as
many of them as possible, and in the evening be driven
from one group to another in a private car, was part of that
same personality.

His spiritual strength, through a great belief in God, is
obvious to all who have contact with him, and this, too,
he did not put above the Polish New Zealanders. In the
homilies he gave after reading the Gospel during a number
of Masses he said in private Wellington homes, "he spoke
from his heart to our hearts a straight-forward message of
faith and love." When, after the consecration of bread, he

raised the Host to lift the Son to the Father, the Cardinal's face was "an expression of pleasure and knowledge."

He is a man of unbounding prayer. A year after his election, he gave priests in Philadelphia a perhaps unintended insight into his mysticism during an address to them about prayer: "No one can effectively bring the good news of Jesus to others unless he himself has been His constant companion through personal prayer, unless he has learned from Jesus the mystery to be proclaimed."

"The greatest contribution you can make in your lives is to communicate Christ to the world," John Paul said in a special address to the young people of Wales in 1982. Even in the papacy, he has lost none of the delight in being with young people which he had back in Poland as a priest and bishop. In the period 1986-95, John Paul attended eight world youth events. He loves the young for their enthusiasm and vitality, their idealism.

The Pope also knows young people can be led astray. "Young people of America," he pleaded in New Orleans in 1987, "let no one deceive you in any way. Don't let yourselves be robbed of hope. Let no one deceive you about the truth of your lives. You young people are proud to live in a free country. You are not really free if you are living under the power of error and falsehood, or deceit or sin. Do not believe anyone who contradicts Jesus or His message which is transmitted to you by the Church. At this point the 'voices' of the world will try to deceive you, with powerful slogans, claiming that you are 'unrealistic,' 'out of it,' 'backward,' even 'reactionary.' But the message of Jesus is clear. Purity means true love, and it is the total opposite of selfishness and escape. The supreme theft in your lives would be if they succeed in robbing you of hope. They will try, but they will not succeed if you hold fast to Jesus and His truth."

•And, yes, while in his late teens at the university in Cracow before the War, Wojtyla did have a steady girlfriend. More than twenty years later, she attended his enthronement as Archbishop of Cracow, and his eyes sought her out in appreciation of her presence.

He has broken all the papal records for foreign travel. This prodigious pastoral impulse includes his becoming, in August 1985, the first pontiff to set foot on Arab soil as an official guest. John Paul went to Morocco where he proposed collaboration on various matters between Christianity and Islam.

Italy's cities and towns, notwithstanding four and a half centuries of successive Italian popes, have also seen more of this pontiff than any other. Milan, the commercial center of Italy, and possessor of many of the riches of Leonardo da Vinci's Renaissance, had not had a papal visit for 500 years till Wojtyla came in 1983.

Nor has language been a barrier to this Polish Peter's ministry. Quite the reverse. That he is probably the best linguist the papacy has had, has universally enhanced his pastoral mission.

Aligned with his spiritual strength was a robust physical strength, acquired from his passionate involvement in the outdoors. In rugby terms, he had the physique "of a good prop forward," to quote another observation from 1973. One of Wojtyla's main concerns after he came to the papacy was whether he would be able to get enough exercise. He quickly mapped out a route which took him daily on more than a mile's walk through the beautifully manicured Vatican gardens. He spied a tennis court and a few days later was playing a game of doubles when light rain started to fall. Both the Pope's partner and their opponents deserted the court, an action the three presumed was the due deference to his Holiness in the circumstances. John Paul stayed put, looked around him with a show of mock amazement, and exclaimed: "We athletes do not mind the rain."

Then he wanted to know from the Curia where the swimming pool was. The Curia replied circumspectly that it could not recollect a previous pope having wanted to swim. So he had a swimming pool built—it was paid for by Polish Americans—at the papal summer residence of Castel Gandolfo outside of Rome in the Alban Hills, which give shelter to the beautiful blue lake the residence overlooks. But his was not a solitary swim. Wojtyla asked members of the papal household and Swiss Guard to pull on their swimming trunks and pile into the pool with him. (Several were reluctant to do so a second time, embarrassed apparently at not being able to keep up with Wojtyla in the water.)

What is perhaps his greatest sporting love, skiing, he seemed to have given up after his election. But in March 1984, skiers at the popular Terminollo winter resort (just north of Rome) thought they might have recognized the Pope skiing incognito on the slopes, moving calmly and turning well. Then four months later, in July, it was official. John Paul spent two days on the slopes of the Adamello mountain range. Tourists were barred for the time, with the exception of the 87-year-old President of Italy, Sandro Pertini, a long time friend, who (in a snow-mobile) accompanied the Pope on the first day. Every year for the next ten years, he skied during a brief winter holiday—but no more. In April 1994, he fell in his private apartment and broke his right leg. He now has an artificial femur, and is having to walk with a cane, which he detests. His humor is still intact, but now he is telling jokes about his age.

When the Pope said Mass at Christchurch during a 1986 tour of New Zealand, he was perhaps further from Rome than he had ever been. At the conclusion of the Mass, John Paul had a question for his large open-air congregation: "What is the distance between Christchurch and Rome?" He answered himself: "At the moment there is no distance." New Zealanders like that sort of humor.

In 1969, shortly after his difficult book, *The Acting Person,* had been published in Poland, Cardinal Wojtyla had had to sit through an overly long sermon by one of his priests. Afterward, the cardinal teased the priest: "Your loquacious tongue will get you into Purgatory." The priest retorted: "And when I get there part of my penance will be to read through your book." Wojtyla doubled up, and it says a fair bit about him that he loved telling that story against himself.

His round face has radiated the inner strength and kindliness of the man. Poles have a saying that round-faced people are very good hearted, and Wojtyla himself has said of people in general: "It's all there in the face."

There is private talk in the Vatican that he has expressed in his will a wish to be buried, not in the crypt under St. Peter's where lie the bodies of popes of recent centuries, but back in his beloved Cracow.

His material possessions are few, mainly some books, icons, and records. His musical enjoyment goes to religious folk songs, and he has liked to sing along in a strong baritone voice.

He watches little television, and only catches the news if it's important. He does take in a little sport on the 'box,' compensation perhaps for the athletic pleasures he can no longer undertake. The Pope well knows the enormous impact the medium has had on society worldwide. "Television can both enrich and harm family life," he wrote in a special 1994 critique.

"It can draw family members close together and foster their solidarity with other families and with the community at large. It can increase their general knowledge and their religious knowledge. But television can harm family life: by propagating degrading values and models of behavior; by broadcasting pornography and graphic depictions of brutal violence; by inculcating moral relativism and religious scepticism; by spreading distorted and manipulative accounts of news; by carrying exploitative advertising; by glorifying false visions of life that obstruct the realization of mutual respect, of justice, and of peace. TV can also isolate family members in their private worlds, cutting them off from authentic interpersonal relations." Parents, the Pope went on, should actively help to form their children's viewing habits.

He is a natural, and deferential talker, and given easily to debate and discussion with his Curia aides on important matters of Church. He consults well with his bishops around the world, and was very much involved with the preparations of the new *Catechism of the Catholic Church*, the first such comprehensive document in more than four centuries.

John Paul's literary output is very large, a task made more considerable by the great amount of travel he has undertaken, with its accompanying homilies and speeches. Toward the end of 1994 came the announcement of *Crossing the Threshold of Hope*, the first book written commercially by a reigning pope for the general public. His publishers, Mondadori, said they expected to sell 20 million copies. (The Pope's royalties go to charity.) It is a small volume, big on hope. Belief in God—"who is silent because He has already revealed everything"—should lead people everywhere "to conquer fear in the present world situation."

Did Wojtyla have a premonition after John Paul I's sudden death that he might be the next pope? Perhaps. He was certainly struck by the fact that the brief, one day conclave which elected Cardinal Albino Luciani, Archbishop of Venice, to succeed Pope Paul VI took place on August 26, which in Poland is the important national feast of Our Lady of Czestochowa, a great favorite of Wojtyla.

Jesus Christ lived on this earth 33 years. Did He, in bringing John Paul I's reign to an end after 33 days, signal how strong was His desire for Wojtyla's pontificate? The Shroud of Turin, a length of linen, has in the past been believed by many to be the burial cloth of Christ, bearing as it does the miraculous image of a man who has been crucified in the detail of the Gospel accounts of Jesus' passion, and whose face has the character authority of a king. 1988 carbon dating seemed to show the cloth was of 12th Century origin (though 1995 research was showing that a fire 400 years ago which scorched the shroud took carbon from the air and chemically bound it to the shroud's fiber—a fact not taken into account in 1988). But the image, and how it got there, remains unexplained by scientific means. In Church sanctioned apparitions during the 1930s to a holy nun, Sr. Pierina, Jesus said of the face on the Shroud: "I firmly wish that my Face reflecting the intimate pains of my soul, the suffering and love of my heart, be more honored. Whoever gazes upon me already consoles me." The Shroud came uniquely into the papal possession of John Paul II at the official start of the 1983 Holy Year. The Shroud, kept in Turin Cathedral since it was transferred 400 years ago from France by the House of Savoy, Italy's former royal family, was willed to the Pope by Italy's last king, Umberto II, who died in exile at Geneva in March 1983.

Indeed, when one looks at this most personable Pope, at what he has performed and what he has proposed, it is almost as though, in these days of danger, God has said to humanity: "Look, here is Pope Karol. This is the best I can do for you."

Chapter 12

A Heavenly Mother

As an ambulance sped him away from St. Peter's Square on that desperate day in May 1981, the shot Pope murmured beseechingly: "Madonna, Madonna."

When he spoke publicly for the first time after the murder attempt, from his hospital bed and via a tape recorder, and in evident pain, his opening words were: "Dear brothers and sisters, I know that in these days, and especially in this moment of the *Regina Coeli* (Queen of Heaven), you are united with me."

He went on to thank all who had prayed for him, to declare he was particularly close to the two people injured also in the attack (a 60-year-old American woman received a bullet through the chest, and a 21-year-old woman from Grenada was shot in the left elbow; both recovered), forgive his attacker, offer his sufferings for the Church and the world, and close with the words: "To you Mary, I say again: *Totus tuus ego sum*—I am entirely yours."

The devotion of Poles to Our Lady is beyond that of possibly any other national people. She is, as mentioned earlier, Queen of Poland, a title of veneration and vow for more than 300 years, culmination of esteem for the womb of Christianity by a people Catholic since 966.

The title "Queen" carries with it the requisite of protector. This property was, in fact, signal to her Polish Queenship. Poland's Marian devotion is centered upon the shrine of Our Lady of Czestochowa, where the famous painting *The Black Madonna* has its home, in the monastery of the Pauline Fathers upon the hill called Jasna Gora ("the mountain of light"). It was toward this hill that Swedish armies in 1655 continued their all-victorious invasion of Poland—"the Deluge" as it's known in Polish history.

Sixteenth and early Seventeenth Century Poland, in federation with Lithuania, had been Central Europe's greatest power. But this power's introduction of an elective, rather than hereditary, monarchy had weakened principal authority. Various candidates for the throne bargained away one royal prerogative after another in search of election. Lutheran Sweden, growing in both military strength and appetite for territory, and particularly seeking control of the Baltic, saw the main chance.

But at the base of the hill Jasna Gora, Sweden suffered its first defeat by the Polish armies. Gradually from then on, the tide turned till peace was signed, with Poland in possession of all its pre-war territory. King Jan Cazimierz went to the Cathedral of Lvov on April 1, 1656, where he placed Poland under the perpetual protection of Our Lady, and declared her Queen of Poland:

"I, Jan Cazimierz, King of Poland, take thee as Queen and Patroness of my kingdom; I put my people and my army under thy protection." This vow was accepted and ratified by both houses of the Sejm (parliament).

Twenty-seven years later, Turkey's Islamic armies thrust their way far into Christian Europe, right to Austria. Strong pleas for help went to Poland's King Jan Sobieski. He prayed first at the Jasna Gora shrine, then, in the name of Our Lady of Czestochowa, led a united Christian army, with a large Polish-Lithuanian contingent, into battle against the Turks, at Vienna. The Turks were trounced, retreated right back to from where they had come, and Christianity in Europe was saved.

The deliverance that is deepest in the Polish psyche is that of 1920. By the second week in August 1920—and less than three years after the bloody, autocratic birth of the Soviet Union—Trotsky's invading Red Army had fought its way west to stand before Warsaw from across the river Vistula. The climactic battle was waged on August 15, Feast of the Assumption of Our Lady. The Poles, under Marshall Jozef Pilsudski, won a comprehensive victory and made safe their sovereignty, and almost certainly that of other East Europeans outside the Soviet Union, for another nineteen years.

The shrine of Our Lady at Jasna Gora continues today to be a united and uniting place of devotion, to which many Polish pilgrims come in transcendent celebration of their powerful Mariology. John Paul II himself said there in 1979: "One must listen in this holy place in order to hear the beating of the heart of the nation in the heart of its Mother and Queen. For her heart beats, we know, together with all the appointments of history, with all the happenings in our national life: how many times, in fact, has it vibrated with the laments of the historical sufferings of Poland, but also with the shouts of joy and victory!" And it was at Jasna Gora on June 18, 1983, that the Pope first used the emotionally charged word "solidarity" during the second homecoming of his pontificate.

Karol Wojtyla was first a part, then a principal in this intense mediation with the Mother of the Son of God. Author George Blazynski, in his book of insight and inspiration, *John Paul II: A Man From Krakow* (Weidenfeld and Nicolson), quotes a Cracow bishop as saying of Wojtyla: "He would go to the sanctuary of the Virgin Mary at Calvary (a Gothic church in Cracow); his father used to take him there when he was a young boy; he would make his way along the roads leading to Calvary as a humble pilgrim countless times; he would come there as a bishop and lay all his troubles before the altar; he would unceasingly lead us to the Virgin Mary and sing her praises...."

The main representation in the coat of arms of Pope John Paul II is a Cross. The second object inserted in the coat of arms is a large, majestic capital M to recall the presence of Mary beneath the Cross and her exceptional participation in the Redemption. The insertion of the M was done at John Paul's insistence, apparently over the protestations of the Church's leading authority on ecclesiastical heraldry who stated an opinion that the use of letters in a papal coat of arms was out of accord with heraldic tradition and diction. Early in his papacy, John Paul declared: "The Pope wishes to entrust the Church particularly to her in whom there was accomplished the stupendous and complete victory of good over evil, of love over hatred, of grace over sin."

In November 1979, the College of Cardinals, apparently without predetermined intent, at a Vatican meeting, dramatically entrusted themselves and the whole Church to the protection of Mary. John Paul welcomed—and made public—this striking invocation a month later, and then quoted from *Genesis* 3:15: *"I will put enmity between thee and the woman, and between thy seed and her seed; it shall bruise thy head and thou shalt bruise its heel."* The Pope elaborating on the word "woman" as Mary, said: "In this difficult age of ours are we not witnesses of this 'enmity'?"

Our Lady is the mother of John Paul's Church by her acceptance of God's will and the power of the Holy Spirit. It is Mary's maternal love that gave the world Christ's love, and motherhood is what Pope John Paul is so greatly fond of expounding when speaking of Mary: "You are a mother. You will understand." His devotion to her is the intimacy of a son's love—he is that close to the Virgin.

In her, for the Pope, is begun the justice and peace which her Son gifted to this earth. John Paul gave an intellectual consideration of this when he visited Lourdes in France to celebrate at this Marian shrine the August 15, 1983, Feast of the Assumption. During a meeting with French President Francois Mitterrand on the vigil of the Feast, the Pope said: "The solution to the world's economic and social difficulties presupposes the fidelity of each to his conscience. Lourdes is precisely this source in which the conscience becomes or 're-becomes' limpid and discovers its first orientation with Mary, so venerated in this country."

Then on the next day, the Feast day, the Pope startled everyone by suggesting that the 2000th anniversary of Mary's birth should be celebrated during the 1983 Holy Year he had proclaimed. There has been a tradition in the Roman Catholic Church that Mary was about 17 when she gave birth to Christ,[1] but no one before had put it as deliberately as the present Pope.

In England, at Wembley Stadium, London, in May 1982, John Paul had again showed his belief in the attention due the Virgin, to the benefit of man: "It is Mary who will teach us how to be silent, how to listen for the voice of God in the midst of a busy and noisy world. It is Mary who will help us find time for prayer. Through the Rosary, the great Gospel prayer, she will help us to know Christ. We need to live as she did, in the presence of God, raising our minds and hearts to Him in our daily activities and worries."

On his first journey abroad as Pope, to Mexico in January 1979, to preside at Puebla over the Third Conference of the Latin American Bishops, John Paul traveled also to the shrine of Our Lady of Guadalupe, north of Mexico City. The shrine, in a basilica, has as its centerpiece a life-sized miraculous portraiture of the Virgin Mary, which for 450 years has played a major role in aiding the Church's mission in Mexico. He said there: "The Pope—who comes from a country in which your images, especially one, that of Jasna Gora, are also a sign of your presence in the nation's life and its hazardous history—is particularly sensitive to this sign of your presence here, in the life of the people of God in Mexico, in its history, a history which has also been not easy, and at times even dramatic."

Just over four years later John Paul paid his first visit to the church of Our Lady of Guadalupe in Rome. There, as he was about to enter, a dove came from nowhere and perched on his hand.

It was to have been expected, therefore, that when the Polish communist party chief—and Soviet directed—General Jaruzelski on December 13, 1981, had brought down the darkness of absolute dictatorship again on Poland, the Pope said in the Vatican: "I have placed Poland in the protection of Our Lady of Czestochowa."

---

1. In her 1917 apparitions at Fatima, Our Lady was about that age, 17, according to those who witnessed the apparitions. In her apparitions before four children in the northern Spanish hillside town of Garabandal during 1961-65, the Virgin indicated to the children that she was 17 when her child, the Christ, was born.

"Love our hearts," Jesus has said of Himself and His mother, and the Pope quickly followed the Holy Year of 1983 with a 1987 special Marian Year. During those two years, 1983 and 1987, by coincidence (or was it?) John Paul made his second and third return pastoral visit to his homeland. When he went the fourth time, in 1991, his great reward from Mary awaited him.

Enthralled by the emotion of the 1987 Marian Year, John Paul created a special prayer for Mary: "The Spirit of God desired you for His mother when He became man to save the human race. You received Him with ready obedience and undivided heart. The Holy Spirit loved you as His mystical spouse, and He filled you with singular gifts. On the eve of the third Christian millennium, we entrust to you the Church which acknowledges you and invokes you as Mother. On earth you preceded the Church in the pilgrimage of faith; comfort her in her difficulties and trials, and make her always the sign and instrument of intimate union with God and of the unity of the whole human race."

The prayer reveres the richness of Mary in John Paul's mind. So often the phrase comes forth from his lips: "You are a mother. . . ." Never, though, was the Virgin a priest, even though she lived to about 57 A.D. If ever there were a person, male or female, truly deserving of the priesthood it was certainly she who brought forth from her own body the Savior of humanity.

The argument concerning women and the Catholic priesthood is most peculiar to our day, and probably most so in the United States. Some of the debate has been along political lines, and therefore has sometimes lacked a perception of the perimeters that do border our God-made institution. They are the words and actions of Jesus, Who, as the wisdom and power of God, was utterly free, confirmed by the Holy Spirit.

Certainly it was a matter aired in the early Church. The great 4th Century apologist St. Epiphanius wrote (in *Against Heresies*): "If women were to be charged by God with entering the priesthood or with assuming ecclesiastical office, then in the New Covenant it would have devolved upon no one more worthy than Mary to fulfill a priestly function. She was invested with so great an honor as to be allowed to provide a dwelling in her womb for the Heavenly God and King of all things, the Son of God.... But he did not find this (the conferring of the priesthood) good. Not even baptizing was entrusted to her; otherwise Christ could better have been baptized by her than John."

John Paul addressed the controversy early in his pontificate, at Philadelphia, during his first visit to America, in October 1979: "The fact that there is a personal individual call to the priesthood given by the Lord to 'the men He Himself had decided on' is in accord with the prophetic tradition. It should help us, too, to understand that the Church's tradition to call men to the priesthood, and not to call women, is not a statement about human rights, nor an exclusion of women from holiness and mission in the Church. Rather, this decision expresses the conviction of the Church about this particular dimension of the gift of priesthood by which God has chosen to shepherd His flock."

But critics, amongst whom a number of American nuns sought a prominence, continued to carry their voice against the Church. Eventually this led the Pope, in May 1994, to issue an apostolic letter, *Ordinatio Sacerdotalis,* in which he used a nearly infallible form of wording to stress the importance of the matter: "Wherefore, in order that all doubt may be removed regarding a matter of great importance, a matter which pertains to the Church's divine constitution itself, in virtue of my ministry of confirming the brethren, I declare that the Church has no authority whatsoever to confer priestly ordination on women, and that this judgment is to be definitely held by all the Church faithful."

That brought no end to the matter for some, and even *Time* magazine, not withstanding its surprise choice of the Pope as its 1994 Man of the Year, in its October 3, 1994 edition, brought a full-page avalanche to the attack, in the name of correspondent Lance Morrow, who exclaimed in an essay that the Pope and bishops "are doomed" for not ordaining women priests. Mr. Morrow, a Catholic, wrote that he had now given up the Eucharist. (Mr. Morrow is of course far from being the only American Catholic to have turned his or her back on the body and blood, soul and divinity of Christ. An April 1994 poll of American Catholics conducted by the *New York Times—CBS News* found that weekly Mass attendance in the 18-29 age group was just 17 percent; for the 30-44 age group it was 35 percent: 45-64, 40 percent; 65 and older, 68 percent.)

Might we be reminded of the Virgin Mary's warning words in 1988 at Medjugorje, in apparition to Fr. Jozo Zovko, the greatest of the priests of that holy place, who relayed her words to Fr. Tim Deeter, an American, that *"a great cloud is descending upon the Catholic Church in America. There are many people who are disloyal to the Holy Father and to the teaching authority of the Church, and without knowing it they are preparing for a schism. People in America will have to decide whom they will follow."*

Chapter 13

The Mother Speaks about Her Pope

The picture of the pontiff was dismaying and distracting. We watched on television, in September 1994, John Paul's arrival by aircraft from Rome in the Croatian capital, Zagreb. He was looking frail and almost ill, having to lean heavily on a walking stick, still in a state of considerable discomfort from the break of his right leg five months previously and the implantation of an artificial femur. At the bottom of the aircraft's steps, unable to kneel in his usual humble gesture on arrival in a foreign country, a bowl of Croatian earth was held to him to kiss.

During the public parts of the 24-hour visit, pain sometimes creased his face. Some of that pain might have been spiritual. He had wanted to be in Sarajevo, capital of tragic Bosnia, two days previously, to bring his love, compassion, and solidarity, in shared suffering, to the populace there. But the Bosnian Serbs would not guarantee his safety. "I plead for peace, harmony, and forgiveness in all of the former Yugoslavia!" he had cried out.

But his physical difficulty, being obvious, led naturally to conjecture about his future. Two years previously he had undergone a difficult operation to remove a large but benign tumor from his intestine. This pontificate was coming to an end, some Catholic scribes opined. The Pope would turn 75 in May 1995, they noted.

Regulations concerning diocesan bishops and archbishops introduced some years back required them, upon turning 75, to submit written resignations to the Holy See, resignations the Vatican can either accept or reject. The circumstances would be suitable for the wearied Pope to resign, on health grounds, after one of the longer reigns in the papacy, and return to his beloved Cracow in retirement, the scribes went on. (Canon Law envisages the possible resignation of a pope. Canon 332:2 says that all that is required for a valid papal resignation is that it be "freely made and properly manifested, but it is not necessary that it be accepted by anyone."—In other words the Pope would not have to re-assemble the College of Cardinals who elected him in order to resign.)

That is assuredly not about to happen.

The apparitions of Our Lady at Medjugorje, in what was then Yugoslavia, began in 1981 on the June 24th feast of St. John the Baptist, precursor of the coming of Christ. The Church was cautious about rendering judgment on the matter, as it is in all such cases, particularly so in this case because the Bishop of Mostar, diocesan capital for Medjugorje, expressed an opinion that the statements of the six young Croatian visionaries that the Mother of God was appearing to them was false. Few now doubt. The miracles, the signs in the sky evocative of the Book of Revelation, and especially the conversions are utterly overwhelming in their numbers.

This small village, bedded in beautiful hues of green, has become one of the great inspirational places of the Church. The parish priest of St. James, Medjugorje, when the visions began, Fr. Jozo Zovko, a Franciscan, was arrested by the communist authorities in 1982 when he refused both to deny the apparitions were taking place and to suppress the visionaries. While in prison he was tortured. Fr. Jozo now lives in a Franciscan monastery about 40 minutes by road from his old parish. Our Lady has appeared to him, too.

The Pope appears to have come early to belief in the apparitions. Medjugorje's new parish priest after Fr. Jozo's arrest, Fr. Tomislav Vlasic, wrote to John Paul in December, 1983, commanded (he said) by the Madonna to advise the Supreme Pontiff "of the urgency and great importance" of the message of Medjugorje. The Blessed Virgin Mary has been telling the visionaries that the whole world is at a critical stage. "She calls repeatedly for reconciliation and conversion. She has warned of a coming chastisement for the sins of the world," Fr. Tomislav said in his letter.

Reports have stated that, on the feast of the Annunciation in 1984, the Pope in Rome met with a friend, Msgr. Paolo Hnilica, who was returning from a visit to Moscow. "Did you come back through Medjugorje, Paolo?" the Pope inquired.

"No, the Curia advised me not to," Msgr. Hnilica said.

"Then go there incognito, and tell me what you saw," John Paul responded keenly. "Medjugorje," the Pope went on, "is the continuation of Fatima."

Subsequently the Pope has met with Fr. Jozo, and with several of the visionaries at different times, in Rome.

Our Lady, in her chosen title, Queen of Peace, on the 25th of each month, gives one of the visionaries Marija Pavlovic Lunetti, a short message for all those who would listen to the voice of Medjugorje. The plea *"pray, pray, pray"* to fight for Jesus against the strength of Satan in the world has been the heart of many of the monthly messages.

The message of August 25, 1994, is extraordinary for Our Lady spoke about John Paul II. The timing was our Blessed Mother's, vigil of the feast of Our Lady of Czestochowa, and less than three weeks before the Pope arrived in Zagreb, where the world would see him in seeming enfeebled state.

The Pope, Our Lady said, is *"my most beloved son, who suffers, and whom I have chosen for these times."*

The phrase *"my most beloved son"* is singular in statement, so firmly rich in its filiality. What does the adjective **most** mean? It means the best, fullest, greatest in quality. And in the expression, we may hear an echo of the Father's words at Jesus' Baptism and Transfiguration.

The phrase *"whom I have chosen for these times"* hardly needs elaboration. In the great contest in the world today between good and evil, Heaven has brought forth its champion, and surely the powers of victory are with that progeny.

The phrase *"who suffers"* takes us back to Our Lady's prophetic 1917 Fatima warning about Russia, and her words near that Portuguese hamlet, that in the finale of her prophecy there would come to the papacy one whom she qualified as: *"He will have much to suffer."* John Paul II had reportedly already tied Medjugorje to Fatima.

His wounding in St. Peter's Square on May 13, 1981, and the 1917 Fatima events seem to have become inseparably linked in the Pope's mind, and he knows well the message for humanity that was delivered by the Virgin in 1917. On June 19, 1983, at the Sanctuary of Czestochowa during his second return home to Poland as Pope, John Paul led the traditional evening singing of the "Call of Jasna Gora," the prayer that the whole Church in Poland offers to Mary every day at the same hour. He left there a part of the white cassock he was wearing on the day of the shooting, the part pierced by the bullet which struck him in the abdomen.

Also in her August 1994 message from Medjugorje, Mary asked all who favor her to pray for the health of the Pope. A month after his journey to Zagreb, the Vatican staged the important Synod on Religious Life in the Modern World. John Paul, noted a participating bishop, attended most of the Synod's sessions, making comments before and at the end of each one. "He has been very jovial and mixes freely at the end of each session," the bishop added.

In March 1995, the Pope resumed weekly visits to Rome parishes—the first time in eleven months—walking up the nave of a church on the Eternal City's outskirts without the need of a cane. At the following month's Palm Sunday (April 9) ceremonies in St. Peter's, John Paul was described as looking "particularly healthy" and spoke forcefully against abortion and euthanasia, subjects of his new encyclical, *Evangelium Vitae* (The Gospel of Life), which was promulgated on March 25, 1995.

There will be no papal resignation in 1995. Great things have come to this pope by the design of Heaven. Great things still await him.

Chapter 14

Why He Was Shot

The horror at the attempt to murder John Paul II in the St. Peter's Square courtyard of his Vatican home before 15,000 pilgrims and tourists on May 13, 1981, was first a compound of humanity's shock at more than a decade of senseless urban terrorism and assassination. This violence had now been taken to its most degenerate end. "It was like shooting God." Indeed, all Christianity, not just one man, seemed struck by the bullets.

The would-be assassin, a 23-year-old Turk and escaped convicted killer named Mehmet Ali Agca, was wrestled to the ground and seized by police. There were disjointed reports in the immediate hours after the shooting of another gunman, pistol in hand, having fled the Square after the Pope fell.

Several days later, when danger to the wounded Pontiff's life had passed, the Vatican's Secretary of State, Cardinal Agostino Casaroli, a man with almost twenty years' diplomatic experience of facing East European regimes on Church matters, said opaquely there might be "another hand" in the attack. Cardinal Casaroli did not elaborate.

When, however, it was learned that the Turk Agca had in November 1979, weirdly threatened to murder Pope John Paul, because he was "the masked leader of the Crusades," just as the Pope was about to begin a historic visit to Turkey to meet the Greek Orthodox Patriarch Demetrius I, there seemed confirmation that the deed in St. Peter's Square was another act of mindless terrorism. During tense interrogation by Italian police, Agca voiced extreme left-wing, then extreme right-wing views. The police announced Agca had insisted to them that he had acted alone in the attack.

Public prosecutor Nicolo Amato carried this view through Agca's trial two months after the shooting, declaring that the Turk had probably acted alone in ideological delirium to try to destroy a highly-placed official. The Rome Assize Courts sentenced Agca to life imprisonment. His first opportunity to plead for parole would not come for twenty-eight years, when he would be aged 51.

It was not until more than three months after the Pope was shot that superb investigative reporting by British Thames journalists for the current affairs *TV Eye* program disclosed a possible, chilling East European management of the attempt to kill John Paul. That Agca, after he had slipped across his country's border into Iran in February 1980, to make good an escape from his Turkish prison, where he was serving a sentence for murder, had sometime later been in communist Bulgaria had become known within 48 hours of his wounding John Paul. But the Turk's time in Bulgaria had been believed to have been short, and investigating Italian police had concentrated inquiries on West Germany, to which Agca also traveled and where there were 1-1/2 million Turkish *Gastarbeiter* (guest workers).

The Thames Television reporters found, however, that Agca had spent several months in Bulgaria in mid-1980—just as Solidarity was coming to fruition—a considerably longer time than initially believed. The reporters were aided by leading Italian journalist Francesco D'Andrea who had had four long briefing sessions with a senior Vatican figure (believed to have been Cardinal Casaroli) about the attempted assassination.

During part of the Turk's time in Bulgaria, which was the Soviet Union's closest ally and was sometimes called "little Russia," he resided in a luxurious hotel in Sofia, the country's capital. All agree that foreigner Agca could not have stayed so long, and so prominently, in this closed country without the knowledge—and acquiescence—of the Bulgarian secret police, who in turn work fraternally and covertly with the Soviet secret police, the KGB.

There, though, the matter lapsed into public silence, not to be resurrected till late in November 1982 by the dramatic arrest of the Bulgarian citizen Sergei Ivanov Antonov, deputy head of the Rome office of Bulgaria's Balkan Airlines, by Italian police. Antonov was remanded in custody on a charge of "active complicity" in the attempted assassination of the Pope. The Bulgarian had worked in Rome for four years.

The ensuing subjective deliberations of the Western press on whether there was now the imprint of a Soviet hand in the assassination attempt invariably were in relation to Poland's Solidarity situation.

Assuredly, the shooting was a Soviet response to a dramatic Polish development on which the presence and popularity of Solidarity concentrated. But its beginning was, rather, in the USSR itself (and here the author can give new information on this serious affair) prior to the birth of Solidarity. This act of Roman Catholicism, unprecedented in Soviet history, Kremlin mentality would have measured as a direct and disturbing challenge to its hegemony.

Lithuania is a small (3½ million population) former Soviet republic on the Baltic sea coast. It shares a southern border and a rich confluent history with Poland. For four centuries (late 14th to late 18th) first dynastically then in formal federation, Poland and Lithuania were one nation. Catholicism[1] was the faith of this nation which became one of the great temporal powers of continental Europe. That power eventually, in mid-18th Century, began to ebb, and by the end of the 18th Century, Lithuania and a large part of Poland had been absorbed into the Russian empire of Catherine II.

Like Poland, Lithuania regained its independence and sovereignty at the end of World War I. The common Catholic culture of these two countries—about 85 percent of

---

1. The Church is the oldest Lithuanian institution, dating back to Christianization in 1387-1413.

Lithuanians were Roman Catholic—made for a strong fel-
lowship again as their huge neighbor, the new USSR,
pushed a brutal atheistic domination over all it could
corral.

At the outbreak of World War II, the Soviet Union rushed
into eastern Poland, seventeen days after Germany invaded
the country from the west (Germany secured the western
half of the country). Lithuania—along with two other Baltic
nations, Latvia and Estonia—fell to a sudden onslaught of
Soviet tanks in June 1940. The Kremlin then declared the
three Baltic nations to be an inalienable part of the USSR.
The Soviets were driven out of the Baltic region the following year, during Germany's broad-front invasion east, but
returned three years later as Germany retreated.

At the end of the war with Germany, the Soviet regime
turned its hand against "the next enemy" in Lithuania, the
Catholic Church. The hierarchy, including the Metropolitan of Lithuania, Archbishop Mecislovia Reinys, was liquidated. The country's three seminaries were closed down,
and one-third of those priests left were exiled. But against
all the odds, Catholicism held on in Lithuania, an act of
great courage and perseverance little remarked on in the
West. The Soviet regime was even forced to reopen one of
the seminaries, at Kaunas (and there were suggestions of
another, underground seminary elsewhere).

Now, about 70 percent of Lithuanians are Catholic. The
retention of religious faith was, of course, inherently hostile to the dictates of the regime. The believer's natural
impulse is truth, because it is the dictate of his or her conscience. This is a freedom that coercion cannot overcome.
God, to Whom the believer was beholden, would always
be a higher authority than the atheistic State. It formed the
basis of the communists' dilemma.

That was the mentality into whose midst a brilliant Catholic priest, Julijonas Steponavicius, began to press in the
early 1950s. The Church made Steponavicius a Bishop in
1955 and appointed him administrator of the Lithuanian
capital's Vilnius diocese. Bishop Steponavicius' adminis-
trative ability and uncompromising faith was met in 1960
by the KGB. The secret police seized the bishop. He was
sent into exile, to the small Lithuanian village of Zagare,

and kept under house arrest. (The regime did not so much as bother with the charade of the staged trial and trumped-up charges, though Article 4 of the Lithuanian Soviet Socialist Republic's Code of Criminal Procedure stated "No one may be prosecuted in any other way than on the basis and procedure established by law.")

The response of the Church came in time. Steponavicius was made Metropolitan of Lithuania, and an Archbishop. Despite this, and despite continuing petitions from priests and laity of the archdiocese to the Kremlin—all unanswered—Archbishop Steponavicius was not released from exile. The regime, by this intransigence, no doubt signaled its belief that the Church career of the Archbishop should be considered concluded.

That the Archbishop's career was at an end was most certainly **not** the view in 1978 of the new East European Pope, the great neighbor from Poland. For immediately after his election, John Paul II had, in a noble and notable act, sent his own Cardinal's red hat to. . .Archbishop Steponavicius. The Kremlin had not recovered from the shock of the election of a Pope from Eastern Europe where the population of Poland, and, nominally, the populations of Hungary and Czechoslovakia, are in the majority Roman Catholic. Then, in virtually the first act of his pontificate, the new Slav pope effectively created the first Soviet resident Cardinal of the Catholic Church since the 1917 Bolshevik Revolution. Not only that, but this Pope made his Cardinal creation in a part of the USSR which, because of the people's strong religious faith, was regarded by the men of Moscow as fundamentally disposed to oppose the dictates of the ruling politburo.

As John Paul's cardinal red hat made its way across the Soviet Union to Steponavicius, it would have burnt a path through the mind of the Kremlin.

Steponavicius' election was in fact an act of solidarity with a historical brother, and a tribute to the steadfastness of the Lithuanian faithful.[2]

---

2. Pope Wojtyla's mother, whose maiden name was Emilia Kaczorowska, was born in the Silesian region of southern Poland, but her family's origins are Lithuanian.

A week before John Paul's mid-June 1983 second homecoming to Poland, the government-controlled Czechoslovak press, which had a reputation for toeing the Soviet line and little else, made a personal attack on the Pope which is revelatory. The Pope had been trying to turn the Church in Eastern Europe into an anti-Soviet third column, the Prague press claimed.[3] That Soviet notion started at the very outset of John Paul's pontificate, and is our first insight into the St. Peter's Square shooting.

In August 1984, the Pope sought to travel to Lithuania to join with Roman Catholics of Vilnius in celebrating the fifth century of the death of St. Casimir, the Polish-born patron saint of Lithuania. The Kremlin gave an emphatic *No* to the request, and refused also to allow Cardinal Casaroli to go in John Paul's place. In a telegram to the Lithuanian Bishops, the Pope called on the country's Catholic community to be "joyful in hope and strong in tribulation."

The Kremlin had a vision of Europe united in concrete communism, and had successfully regimented half the continent to this resolution. Western societies were perceived by Moscow as being weakened by permissiveness which would, in time, render more readily their peoples to the ambitions of Soviet autocracy. The primary proviso to this was home base—Eastern Europe—being kept intact.

Pope John Paul had a continental vision too—a magnanimous and majestic vision of a Europe united in the liberty and love of Christ. While the Kremlin looked west for the accomplishment of its goal, John Paul reached more naturally to Europe's eastern half, to the Soviets' home base, with his message of the mission of Christ. The Pope is from the east, and counsels Roman Catholicism's reconciliation with schismatic Orthodoxy with more compelling immediacy than reconciliation with the separated Protestant Churches of the West.

---

3. In 1985 Pope John Paul wanted to travel to Czechoslovakia to join with Catholics of that country in tributes to St. Methodius, who helped convert the Slavs to Christianity, in what was the 1100th anniversary of the saint's death. The Prague government replied that the Pope could only come in a private capacity and that the government could not be responsible for his safety. John Paul did not go.

Orthodox Christians are mainly Slavs—there are various patriarchates: they include Russia, Bulgaria, Georgia, Constantinople, Antioch, and Rumania—a race dominated by its Russian part. The Pope is a Slav, and at Gniezno in Poland, in June 1979, with the vivid word imagery he is so capable of, John Paul became the portentous Pope of the Slavs.

He spoke on June 3, the Feast of Pentecost, and reminded the huge crowd around him at Mass outside the cathedral in the town square, that the descent of the Holy Spirit upon the Apostles that day in the Jerusalem upper room marked the beginning of the Church. One of the Holy Spirit's gifts to the Apostles was to fill them with the ability to speak other languages, John Paul went on. "Today, on this anniversary, as we go back to those beginnings, we cannot fail to hear also, as well as the language of our forefathers, other Slav languages and related languages, languages in which there then began to be heard the voice of the upper room that was opened wide to history. These languages cannot fail to be heard especially by the first Slav pope in the history of the Church."

Was it not Christ's will, was it now what the Holy Spirit disposed, he asked, "that this Pope, in whose heart is deeply engraved the history of his own nation, from its very beginning, and also the history of the brother peoples and the neighboring peoples, should in a special way manifest and confirm in our age the presence of these peoples in the Church and their specific contribution to the history of Christianity?"

He did not flinch: "Is it not Christ's will, is it not what the Holy Spirit disposes, that this Polish Pope, this Slav Pope, should at this precise moment manifest the spiritual unity of Christian Europe? Yes, it is Christ's will, it is what the Holy Spirit disposes." Those words could only be regarded by the militant atheists of the Kremlin as a challenge to their regime.

Then, late in November of that same year, 1979, John Paul consolidated the path he was traveling with a momentous meeting in Turkey with the Ecumenical Patriarch of Constantinople, Dimitrios I, the senior of the Patriarchs of the fourteen Orthodox Churches, with authority to speak for them all. Rapport between the two quickly became obvious. The Pope and the Patriarch attended each other's liturgies, the first time this had been done since the great schism of A.D. 1054.[4]

John Paul told the Ecumenical Patriarch that unity between Catholicism and Orthodoxy would be a fundamental and decisive step in the progress of the entire ecumenical movement. The schism had not been without influence on later divisions, he said—a reference to the Protestant Reformation. The Pope went on: "The visit I am making today is intended as an encounter in the apostolic faith we share, so that together we might journey towards the full unity which has been damaged by unfortunate historical circumstances. What else should we do but express our firm hope in God that a new era will soon begin? On that account, Your Holiness, I am happy to be here today to express the profound respect and the sense of fraternal solidarity felt by the Catholic Church for the Eastern Orthodox Churches."

The following day, November 30, the Feast of St. Andrew, the Apostle brother of St. Peter, John Paul and Patriarch Dimitrios signed a joint declaration to set up a bilateral committee for theological dialogue. The Patriarch expressed his strong support for eventual full communion, and added: "Our ultimate goal is not simply the unity of our two Churches but the union of all Christians in the one Lord and in participation in the same cup."

The warmth and regard the Patriarch and Pope held for each other was demonstrated by the swiftness with which the bilateral committee got to work. Just six months after the joint declaration's signing, the committee held its first sessions (they spanned a week, May 29 to June 4, 1980), on the islands of Patmos and Rhodes.[5]

The largest of the Eastern Churches, the Russian Ortho-

---

4. The split between Byzantine and Roman Christianity.
5. The pace of this work continued to an extent that, after a meeting in the Vatican in June 1984 between the Syrian Orthodox Patriarch of Antioch, Ignatius Zakka I Iwas, and John Paul, a joint declaration stipulated that should the laity of either faith be without access to a priest of their own Church, they can receive the sacraments of Penance, the Eucharist and, if they need, the Anointing of the Sick, from a priest of the other Church.

dox Church, which the Soviet communists believed they controlled, was of course joined in these talks. The antagonistic Kremlin brooded in the background, saying little.

Then two and a half months later, there came from Catholic Poland, the especial place of the Pope, the great challenge to the Kremlin's post-War hegemony of Eastern Europe, Solidarity. Things were happening, fast—unprecedented things.

Of course Pope John Paul II was the spiritual head of Solidarity. When the freedom strikes erupted in the Gdansk shipyard in August 1980, John Paul was at his Castel Gandolfo summer residence. The Pontiff and some close Polish friends gathered around a television set to watch the first film reports of the shipyard strikes. The scenes were initially of the faces of angry workers, then the camera zoomed in on a bright object hanging on the shipyard gates: a portrait of the Pope. "His face froze and his lip stiffened," one of the Pontiff's friends present, Rev. Josef Zycinski, later recalled for *Newsweek* magazine. "He tried not to react, but we all saw its impact on his face." The next day the friends saw tears in John Paul's eyes as he dedicated a Mass to his native Poland.

On November 10, 1980, the Soviets had to watch the Polish communist regime agree to the formal ratification and legal registration of Solidarity as the first free trade union federation in the Marxist history of East Europe, and two days later listen to John Paul in the Vatican express his "joy" at "this wise and mature agreement."

In January 1981, Solidarity's leader Lech Walesa made his first trip abroad, to the Vatican for a papal audience. Walesa met the man whose writings and preachings during his episcopate had helped begin the progression to Solidarity. Now it was the presence of this dynamic Polish Pope, his singular endeavor to move East European minds to the higher properties—and prerogatives—of life, and the sense he had given them of himself as a man of destiny, that was helping vitally to sustain Solidarity.

And then, suddenly, in mid-April 1981, there came a major crisis to the Kremlin which brought the matters of John Paul II to a head. It became public knowledge in

Poland that the country's 79-year-old Cardinal Primate, Stefan Wyszynski, was dying of stomach cancer. The Cardinal had little more than a month to live, it was believed.

Death was coming to the man who had for three decades as Primate been indomitable in Polish Church affairs. This was not important to the Kremlin. What was important—all important—was that surely the inspired Polish son who had come to the papacy from the position of Deputy Primate would return to Poland to administer the last rites of the Church to Cardinal Wyszynski. John Paul had immediately after his election written publicly to Cardinal Wyszynski: "Venerable and beloved Cardinal Primate, allow me to tell you just what I think. The Polish Pope who today full of fear of God, but also of trust, is beginning a new pontificate, would not be on Peter's chair were it not for your faith which did not retreat before prison and suffering, were it not for your heroic hope. . . ."

How would the Polish people in their emotionally charged atmosphere receive back their papal son? As the final liberator?

A week after knowledge of the Primate's impending death became public, the Soviet Politburo's senior member and hardline chief ideologist, Mikhail Suslov, rushed from Moscow to Warsaw with a hundred henchmen on an unscheduled visit to personally assess the mood of the Polish people. He met the ineffectual Polish communist chairman, Stanislaw Kania, against whom Solidarity had a succession of successes.[6] A brief Soviet statement, issued as the delegation departed back to Moscow, was significant only for the absence of the "identity of views" usual after such inter-East European meetings.

What the members of the Soviet Politburo—thirteen men of autocratic and atheistic power under the leadership of Leonid Brezhnev—now faced would, to them, have been the climax of Catholic encroachment by a Pope uniquely of Slavic origin and salient achievement. Would they still be holding Poland, the second largest nation of their

6. And who was desposed in October 1981 by the nation's Premier, General Jaruzelski.

empire, after the return home of this man to the rites of Cardinal Wyszynski?

It was not so much a question of a deliberate, determined *putsch* in Warsaw, rather more a matter of communists in Poland, outnumbered thirty to one by Poles opposed to their ideology, simply being swept aside as Catholic Solidarity emotionally raised its Pope to a sovereign Polish pinnacle. There was no strong Soviet armed presence in Poland. The 315,000-member Polish Armed Forces, with the exception of the mostly communist officers, reflected Catholicism's overwhelming popular presence.

One million Soviet troops would have been needed to try to re-take Poland. Would they have dared invade with massive onslaught and carnage in the presence of the Pope, as the whole world watched? And without response from the nominally Christian West?

Even with the Pope departed back to the Vatican, the essentials of such a conflict would not have changed.

And what would be the effect on Hungary and Czechoslovakia, whose opposition to Soviet rule was, by historical example, and remained deep in the psyches of their people, whose Catholicism had been reignited by the Slav Pope? And what would be the effect on Catholic Lithuania, with its close family and historical associations with Poland and common border? And on Latvia, which sits atop Lithuania on the Baltic and has a significant, minority Catholic population? Here we were talking about the USSR itself. And in Ukraine that vast south Russian area with a border on Poland, where anti-Soviet nationalism remained strong, where a large "catacomb" Catholic Church with its own clandestine bishops and priests existed and for whose people the Pope, in October 1979, at the Ukrainian Church of the Immaculate Conception in Philadelphia, courageously expressed his high esteem, "I have known of the many sufferings and injustices you have endured."

It is no exaggeration to say that by the last week of April 1981, the stakes for the Kremlin had become very, very high.

On April 25, the Turk Agca arrived on the Mediterranean island of Majorca. There he waited.

In the Vatican, preparations for John Paul's trip home began. It had been agreed that to comfort and make splendid the Cardinal Primate, the public announcement from Rome that the Polish Peter was to lead the funeral rites would be made before Wyszynski's death.

On May 10, Agca arrived in Rome. He took a room in a nondescript boarding house fifteen minutes' walk from St. Peter's Square. A Browning 9-mm semi-automatic pistol and several cartridge clips had been given to him.

Agca shot John Paul in St. Peter's Square on May 13, almost certainly the last day the general public had access to the Pope before he was to have announced his intention to return to Poland.

Barely two weeks after the shooting, Cardinal Wyszynski died of his cancer.

On June 16, 1983, the Supreme Soviet—it was called the country's parliament, though its members were appointed by the Communist Party hierarchy—met in formal session. Since such sessions are few in a year, it is reasonable to assume it was no coincidence that this was the day on which John Paul II would fly from Rome to Warsaw to start the second pastoral visit to his homeland. The new Soviet leader, Yuri Andropov, at that session, called for closer political and economic integration between the communist states of Eastern Europe. "To strengthen the co-operation and cohesion between these countries is, I would say, the paramount aim of the international activities of the Soviet Communist Party," he said. In other words, the Kremlin's first priority is keeping home base intact.

Andropov was followed to the rostrum by Andrei Gromyko, Soviet Foreign Minister since 1957. "Poland," Gromyko stated, "has been and will remain an indivisible part of the socialist community.

"Only a person blinded by hopelessly fossilized hostility to socialism (a derogatory Soviet term for an advocate of God) can fail to see this."

Gromyko went on: "The Soviet bloc has shown more than once, in word and deed, that it is capable of dealing with all those who interfere with its movement forward and all attempts to harm the legitimate interests of this community and test its firmness."

Those words were spoken, it is to be emphasized, as

Pope John Paul was departing for Warsaw. Gromyko could not have made himself plainer.

Just hours after he arrived in Poland's capital, John Paul told a large congregation in St. John Cathedral at a Mass in honor of Cardinal Wyszynski, that he had intended to return to Warsaw in May 1981, but he had been unable to because of the attempt on his life.

The Pope said he would have been in Warsaw for the Cardinal's funeral on May 31. That meant he would have been in the Polish capital in the immediate aftermath of the funeral, when the death, laying in state in the cathedral for three days, and burial had been done with and Polish emotions free. He also said in Warsaw at this time: "I want Poland between East and West."

The arrest of the Bulgarian Sergei Antonov was apparently the result, initially, of information in a letter Agca wrote to Cardinal Casaroli after a year in prison. The contents of the letter were reported to Italian police, and Agca then called for an Italian judge to hear a full confession of his knowledge of the assassination conspiracy.

Italian police investigators went to Agca's cell in Rebibbia Prison outside Rome and handed him photographs of one hundred different individuals, including two Bulgarians Agca had now named, Antonov and Jelio Vassilev. The investigators asked the Turk to point out the faces of the two Bulgarians. Agca sifted through the photographs and unerringly drew out those of Antonov and Vassilev.

Agca named a third Bulgarian as an accomplice, Todor Aivazov. Given the mentality affected by the Turk under police questioning immediately after he shot the Pope, the actions of Rome police were governed now by what Agca could indubitably show to be true. Agca supplied the investigators with details of the Bulgarians' homes, furnishings, and cars that could only have been known from intimate contact.

Immediately after reports of Antonov's arrest, Aivazov, an accountant at the Bulgarian Embassy in Rome, went back to Bulgaria. Aivazov had been stationed in the Italian capital since before the Pope's shooting.

Vassilev, who had been an assistant to the Bulgarian Embassy's military attaché in Rome, apparently with the rank of Major when John Paul was wounded, had returned to Sofia in mid-1982.

The Italian Foreign Ministry revoked the diplomatic status of Vassilev and Aivazov, and arrest warrants were issued. The warrants remain outstanding.

Two Turkish nationals, though, were arrested late in 1982 in connection with the conspiracy: Omar Bagci in Switzerland, and Musa Cedar Celibi in West Germany, and extradited to Italy. The name of another Turk, Oral Celik, was later also to be spoken, and it was even posited that he was in St. Peter's Square at the time of the shooting.

Italian police sources said that Agca had begun an association with Turkish criminals in Sofia after his escape from prison. The criminals, involved mainly in smuggling, and led by a Turk named Bekir Celenk, worked with the connivance of the Bulgarian regime.

The police sources at this time, and Church sources, also gave details of Agca's confession. He said that on both May 11 and 12, 1981, he was driven to St. Peter's Square by Antonov and Vassilev to select the most suitable site for the assassination attempt.

On the morning of May 13, the fateful day, the Turk was taken by car to Vassilev's home in the outer Rome suburb of Tor Di Quinto. Antonov was already there. Agca had the Browning pistol with him. Vassilev took two pistols from his home, and a concussion grenade, Agca said, which was to be used to create crowd confusion after the Turk had shot the Pope.

Vassilev gave one of the pistols to Antonov, who drove Agca to St. Peter's Square for the afternoon murder attempt, parking the car outside the Canadian Embassy to the Holy See in the Via della Conciliazione, the main thoroughfare into the Vatican.

Antonov remained in the Square after the shooting, but apparently Vassilev did not. The Rome Bulgarian Embassy denied that Antonov had been anywhere near St. Peter's Square on the day of the shooting. But a re-examination of dramatic news photographs taken in the Square seconds after the shooting clearly showed in one the face of Antonov straining expectantly over the head of one person in front of him toward the wounded Pontiff, slumped on the popemobile in the arms of John Paul's Polish-born secretary and close friend, Monsignor Stanislaw Dziwisz, a mere four yards from Antonov. The Bulgarian's features are sharp and sure.[7]

In December 1982, Stefan Svredlev, who as a colonel in the Bulgarian secret police had defected to the West some years previously, repeated publicly what he had told the Western intelligence personnel immediately after his defection—that his country's secret services, in their international operations, followed the directives of the Soviet KGB which had officers in every sector of the Bulgarian organization.

Alexandre de Marenches, head of French intelligence in 1981 before his retirement, then surprised everyone by publicly revealing that he had solid evidence, in late April 1981, that an Eastern bloc assassination attempt against the Pope was imminent. So confident was he of his information that he had sent two deputies to the Vatican to warn papal aides.

Two days after Christmas 1983, in the Holy Year of reconciliation and repentance proclaimed by John Paul II, the Pope and Agca met in Agca's prison cell—the victim to forgive again his attacker, the assailant to ask his victim's forgiveness. As the Pope observed to women inmates of the prison later: "Providence has taken things into its own hands, in what I would call an extraordinary way."

For twenty-one minutes John Paul and Agca sat in chairs faced close to each other in front of the cell's radiator and whispered into each other's ears. The atmosphere was confessional. Once Agca was seen to brush tears from his eyes. After he departed the cell, John Paul told waiting reporters: "I spoke with a brother of ours in whom I have complete trust. What we told each other is a secret between us."

In April 1984, Italian State Prosecutor Antonio Albano completed a lengthy probe into the assassination attempt. Albano recommended the prosecution of Antonov, Vas-

---

7. The photograph is shown to perhaps its best effect on Page 175 of Lord Longford's biography *Pope John Paul II*. Longford's book was published before the Bulgarian connection had been established, and almost a year before Antonov's arrest.

silev, and Aivazov (the latter two Bulgarians in absentia), of the two Turkish nationals in custody, and several other Turks in absentia, on charges of complicity in the attempt to murder John Paul.

Six months later, at the end of October 1984, Judge Ilario Martella formally indicted the three Bulgarians, the two Turks in custody, Bagci and Celibi, the Turk suspected of being in the Square with Agca at the time of the shooting, Celik, whose whereabouts were not known, and the Turk Celenk, believed to be in Bulgaria.

On May 28, 1985, the scene and sense for Mehmet Ali Agca changed most dramatically. No longer was there the solitude and privacy of the informant's Rebibbia Prison cell or the state prosecutor's office for interview. Now he was in the very public presence of many international press members in a courtroom called "the Bunker," a converted Rome gymnasium with a metal fence around it, guard towers at its corners, closed circuit television, and many armed guards about it. No longer the friendship of the state prosecutor, now the penetrating questions of the trial prosecutor, Antonio Marini, and of the defense counsel.

The events and historical consequences had impacted upon Agca's mind—immature when he shot and wounded John Paul II. Now in this substance and setting that mind swung from the bizarre to the haltingly rational.

"I am Jesus Christ!" the Turk shouted on that first day of the trial. "I am omnipotent, I announce the end of the world!" A month later he said to the Judge, Severino Santiapichi: "I will bring back to life a person who is scientifically dead, provided the Vatican acknowledges I am Jesus Christ."

When he began to talk slowly, and with seeming sense—for there were matters of follow-up that were palpable—about a meeting in the Bulgarian capital of Sofia with a Soviet diplomat in July 1980, the Soviet Embassy in Rome tersely dismissed it as "Agca's usual fantasies."

Indeed, the way Agca's mind could swerve into dementia gave the Soviet and Bulgarian regimes the "out," and made almost academic—except for the Turkish and Bulgarian defendants—the trial's verdicts when they would come. Agca was, after all, the state's principal prosecution witness.

The Turk Bagci took the stand in his own defense to admit that four days before the assassination attempt—and the day before Agca arrived in Rome—he had given Agca a package in Milan. Bagci said he was 90 percent certain the package contained a firearm, but claimed he had never opened the package which he had brought from Switzerland.

In his testimony to the court, the Bulgarian Antonov denied he had driven Agca to St. Peter's Square on May 13, 1981. "In fact, I have never met the person who accuses me," Antonov said.

Early in July, Bulgaria startled the prosecution by releasing to Turkish custody Bekir Celenk, who was being tried in absentia on the complicity charge. Subsequently, a Turkish prosecutor in an Ankara court demanded the death penalty for Celenk on charges of smuggling arms and drugs. But on the eve of the seventh anniversary of John Paul II's election as Pope, Turkish authorities announced Celenk's death from a heart attack.

Agca's evidence about his meeting in Sofia in July 1980 with a Soviet diplomat was revelatory. The Russian he named was Malenkov, First Secretary at the Soviet Embassy in the capital. The diplomat met him and three other Turkish terrorists—including Celenk—in Room 911 of the Hotel Vitosha in Sofia. There the First Secretary offered 3 million West German marks for the assassination of the Pope, Agca told the court.

When the Judge himself challenged the Turk on this, Agca responded: "I ask the court to show me photographs of all the personnel of the Soviet Embassy in Sofia. I will surely recognize him." The immediacy with which Agca had removed the photographs of Bulgarians in Rome from those of an assortment of other individuals in 1982 had impressed Italian Police. Agca went on to describe to the court the alleged Soviet conspirator, whose Christian name he did not know: "The diplomat was 5 feet 11 inches tall, with a long and full face, wearing glasses, blond hair, and of a sporting appearance." Again, the details of the Bulgarians he had given in 1982, particulars he could only have known from intimate contact, had further impressed Italian Police.

Malenkov, Agca said, also discussed bombing the United States-financed Radio Free Europe in Munich which broadcasted to Eastern Europe news not available to Slavs through the communist-censored media.

In fact, a bomb badly damaged the premises of Radio Free Europe, in February 1981, injuring eight people.

That the Soviet regime seemingly had it in mind before the advent of Poland's Solidarity to murder John Paul II shows how strong the Pope's influence in Eastern Europe was perceived to be by the Kremlin.

However, while it was the Soviets who offered the payment for the Pope's murder, it was the Bulgarian diplomat Vassilev, in his Rome Embassy's military attaché office, who provided Agca with details about the Pope's weekly routine, the Turk continued in evidence. "It was also Vassilev who suggested I write the letter found upon myself in St. Peter's Square after I had shot the Pope in which I said I was shooting the Pope to protest about United States and Soviet imperialism. He said that, in the event of my capture, it would be useful to give the impression that I was acting alone."

The trial continued in fits and starts till Easter 1986, when the verdict was given. The judge, his deputy, and six lay jurors found that there was "not sufficient evidence" to convict the defendants on the complicity to murder charge.

The verdict was unsurprising, given the prosecution's principal reliance on Agca. According to Italian legal sources quoted by Reuter, the acquittal formula applied meant that the eight-person jury felt a case might still exist against the Bulgarians and Turks, but had not been sufficiently proved to warrant a conviction. Bagci was found guilty, however, of illegally importing the pistol Agca used in his attack on John Paul, and sentenced to three years in prison, which he did not have to serve under his terms of extradiction from Switzerland. Antonov returned to Sofia.

The Kremlin, no doubt believing it was having the last word, said through Moscow's Tass news agency: "The claims of a communist plot to kill the Pope have crumbled to nothing."

Chapter 15

Heaven's Response

Between the 1981 shooting of the Pope and Moscow's quaint claim at the end of the Rome trial, there were five short years. Another five short years later, on May 13, 1991—and a decade to the day since the 1981 shooting— John Paul II stood at the prophetic shrine of Fatima.

Prelates and many faithful surrounded him. In the evening, though, he returned privately to the shrine, stayed there, and prayed at great length.

He had been to Fatima before as Pope. That was back in 1982, to thank the Virgin for having kept him alive during the assassination attempt on that dreadful day the previous year. Now he was here as a Pope of some triumph. Central and much of eastern Europe had been liberated from the atheistic datum and dictatorship of Russia.

In a few weeks he would physically return to a free Poland. Fatima, the great revelator of Russia, was declared by John Paul, on his second visit there, to be the Marian capital of the world. And Our Lady had pledged herself to this Pope with all the power and prophecy of Fatima. So like central and parts of eastern Europe, neither the Soviet Union nor a communistic Russia could remain, no matter how huge might be Moscow's military hand.

Out of Fatima it came....Let us follow in the Virgin's steps. They are easy to see and quite precise.

The Fatima seer, Sr. Lucy (Lucia), in an October 1992 interview granted to several prelates of the Church (including Cardinal Antony Padiyara of Ernaculam, India) at the convent of St. Teresa in Coimbra, Portugal, said the Soviet Communist Party chief Mikhail Gorbachev had unknowingly been an instrument of God. That instrumentation had almost come to an end, though, in August 1991.

Communist hardliners, including the Soviet Defense Minister Yazov, KGB chairman Kryuchkov, Interior Minister Pugo, and Prime Minister Pavlov, had ordered Gorbachev and his wife Raisa and important aides seized at the Gorbachevs' Crimean coast holiday residence in an attempted coup.

The coup failed—and there must not go unacknowledged the courage at this time of Russia's democratically elected President, Boris Yeltsin, standing atop a Soviet tank in front of Moscow's Russian Parliament building in defiance.

Upon his release, a furious Gorbachev returned to Moscow from the Crimea after 80 hours of captivity, sat down at his Kremlin desk, and wrote a decree disbanding the Communist Party. The date was August 22—feast of the Queenship of Our Lady.

The part of the USSR most stubborn and splendid in its Catholic faith, the Baltic states of Lithuania, Latvia, and Estonia, then gained their sovereign independence by Gorbachev's pen. Independence day was September 8—Birthday of Our Lady.

The Ukraine, Roman Catholic in its western half, had declared its national sovereignty in July of the previous year—but Gorbachev in Moscow had not accepted that the Kremlin no longer had rule over this large European land, almost the size of France. That 1990 sovereignty declaration had drawn strength perhaps by the Ukrainian rite Catholic Church, a short time previously having "come out from the catacombs." The rite's bishops, priests, and religious had openly declared themselves. The Pope, in a 1989 speech, had been particularly firm on the right to legal recognition and to full religious freedom of the Ukrainian Catholic Church.

In June 1990, the Pontiff, with great warmth and affection, had greeted the Ukrainian-resident bishops in the

Vatican, the first open meeting of the bishops outside the Ukraine since the rite's suppression in 1946.

With the Archbishop of Lvov, there were all of ten bishops—which showed just how strong the Church there had remained under persecution. "We owe this meeting to God Himself," John Paul told the bishops. "I ask you in your Ukrainian homeland to foster reconciliation in the style of Christ."

Now it was December 1991, and Gorbachev was acceding to Ukrainian demands—indeed was throwing in the whole towel. Leaders of the three large Slav republics of Russia, Ukraine, and Belarus met at Minsk to launch the Commonwealth of Independent States. It was the eighth day of December, Feast of the Immaculate Conception.

The final act of the year's great Marian drama before Gorbachev left the political stage was his formal announcement of the dissolution of the USSR, and the lowering of the hammer and sickle flag from the Kremlin masthead—on the Eve of Christmas, when the Virgin Mary brought forth the Savior of the world.

"Your spirit rejoices, O Mary," the Pope said in an August 15, 1993, Feast of the Assumption homily, "and our spirit rejoices with you, because the Mighty One has done great things for you, and for us, and holy is His name."

Chapter 16

The Finale of Fatima

John Paul II is the first Slav pope. He comes from that race which includes Russians, Poles, Silesians, Croats, Bulgarians, Czechs, and Bohemians. We already have a dramatic perception of this fact from previous chapters.

There has, of course, been a prophecy about a Slav pope—given 130 years before Karol Wojtyla's election to St. Peter's chair. It came from the pen of a fellow Pole, Juliusz Slowacki, one of Poland's three great 19th Century poets.

Slowacki wrote, in 1848, that:

> When dangers abound Almighty God
> Heaves on a great bell-rope,
> And opens His throne
> To a new Slav Pope...
>
> His face will shine forth
> Like a lamp in the dark,
> And lead growing generations
> To the light of God's ark...
>
> To support God's world
> Needs strength and hope,
> So behold our brother
> The new Slav Pope...

Just as nations turn to guns
So love will be his arm,
And the Sacraments his power,
As the world lies in his palm. . . .

During the early years of the Second World War, Mrs.
Irena Szkocka of Cracow, whom Karol Wojtyla came to
know so well and appreciate so greatly that he virtually
adopted her as his grandmother, wrote alongside the lines
of that poem: "This Pope will be Karol." Mrs. Szkocka
died at the age of 92 in 1971, when he, Karol, was aged
51, and already a Cardinal of four years' standing.

Given the wonderful manner of Wojtyla's mind, his
achievements among the Slav people—their release from
atheistic domination—his great apostolic movement
throughout the world, and the other signs of his grace that
have been before us, few would doubt the wisdom of Mrs.
Szkocka given more than 50 years ago.

Few also would doubt the power of the Fatima prophecy,
made almost 80 years ago, and Wojtyla's place as Pope in
it. John Paul has, after all, himself laid his name upon this
particular appellation of Our Lady.

That the Fatima prophecy has been fulfilled in much of
its warning and promise gives it a proof and force of
authenticity. That the prophecy was made by the Blessed
Virgin Mary, and followed by a promised public miracle
of celestial proportions before 70,000 witnesses might be
said to be the mark of its omnipotence.

But we must now consider if, after the astonishing events
of 1989-91, the prophecy of Fatima—Heaven's potent warning for the 20th Century—is complete and the world has
moved beyond it.

The prophecy is the one delivered by the Blessed Virgin
Mary during a series of apparitions before three children
at Fatima in Portugal. The Mother of Christ warned in
mid-1917 of a Russia about to rise, whose character and
course would be anti-man and anti-God; a Russia *"which
will spread her errors throughout the world arousing wars,
and persecutions of the Church. Many good people will be
martyred."* The punishment of the world for its great sins
was at hand, she said.

Our Lady proceeded that there would come to the papacy

a Holy Father who *"will have much to suffer"*—and John Paul II's place in these events was first manifested by the fact that the 1981 day he suffered those grievous gunshot wounds in St. Peter's Square, May 13, was the anniversary of the first of the Fatima apparitions, and the day on which priests who wish to mark Fatima by a Mass celebration do so.

The Virgin Mary then gave a warning of appalling destruction—making it part of our fears today of nuclear war—and went so far as to say: *"Some nations will be annihilated."*

However, she also spoke some relief: *"In the end my Immaculate Heart will triumph. The Holy Father will consecrate Russia to me. Russia will be converted, and there will be some peace."* This will have to be part of our consideration, in a little while: Has Russia now been converted, and does the world have a proper perception of the greatness and generosity of God who has worked such wonders in our recent world?

That is the sequence of the prophecy. Before we look at the circumstances of the apparitions, it is necessary that, to establish the sense of the first half of the prophecy, we acknowledge some unpleasant statistics. Ivan Kurganov, emigre Professor of Statistics from Leningrad University, in a work of calculation which remains the classic of its kind, measured that, discounting war casualties, between the years 1917 and 1959 some 66½ million Soviet citizens were killed in the name of communism. Professor Kurganov published his 2,500-word report, in March 1964, in the New York-based Russian language journal, *Novoye Russkoye Slovo.*

Alexander Solzhenitsyn, Russia's greatest living writer, and resolute opponent of the Soviet regime, used Professor Kurganov's calculation as sole reference in his famous *Letter to Soviet Leaders,* written in September 1973, for the horrific number of people in the USSR who died unnatural deaths. Solzhenitsyn himself, in his epic history of the vast compass of USSR political prisoners' labor camps, *The Gulag Archipelago,* estimated that, between December 1917 and the mid-1950s, some 50 million workers were held by the Gulag, up to half of whom died there.

Pope John Paul II himself, when he spoke to the United Nations General Assembly in October 1979, reminded delegates that the previous June he had visited Auschwitz, and went on: "This infamous place is unfortunately only one of the many scattered over the continent of Europe."

This regime, which became the deadliest opponent of man, at the outset of its rule, determined to expunge religion from its realm. "Every idea of God is unutterable vileness, vileness of the most dangerous kind, contagion of the most abominable kind," Lenin said.

Priests and people of religious orders, places of prayer and worship were made a main enemy. The persecution of the Orthodox and Catholic churches was particularly violent. "Twenty bishops and hundreds of priests of the Orthodox Church have been murdered by Soviet communists during 1918," the Vatican angrily declared in April 1919.

Dr. Georg von Rauch, West German Professor of Russian History, wrote in his 1957 *A History of Soviet Russia* that there were some statistics indicating that altogether 28 archbishops and bishops and 6,775 priests were killed there during Lenin's years of power.

In 1922 alone, according to Nikita Struve in his thoroughly researched *Christians in Contemporary Russia* (Harvill Press), "2,691 secular priests, 1,962 monks, and 3,447 nuns were liquidated."

Churches' lands were seized, ecclesiastical schools, seminaries, and monasteries were closed by the regime. In 1917, the Catholic Church had 980 churches and chapels open in Russia, according to Struve. By 1934, only three remained open. In 1917, there were twenty-one Catholic bishops and apostolic administrators; by 1934, none.

Religion in the USSR won back considerable freedom in the wake of the 1941 German invasion. Stalin, needing to promote every support now that his regime was in mortal danger, allowed hundreds of Orthodox priests to come out of hiding, monastic life to be restored, religious communities to be reformed, and many churches to be reopened. But with the war won, persecution returned. We have seen what happened in Lithuania. In the Ukraine, the Catholic Archbishop of Lvov, Josyf Slipyi, and ten other bishops were cast into prison, and so on in its horror.

As the Soviet regime extended its empire throughout Eastern Europe in the post-War years, the persecutions of the predominant Roman Catholic faith rivaled those of Lenin's years.

In 1959, the Soviet Communist Party under Khrushchev's leadership began a campaign it hoped would achieve the final extinction of religion in the country. As many of the churches, monasteries, and nunneries still open from the War years were compelled to close—several of the most beautiful cathedrals in the country were blown up—priests without churches as a consequence were informed they could no longer minister to the faithful. In 1961, the communists murdered Nicholas, Metropolitan of Krutitsy, the second most important figure in the Russian Orthodox Church.

In May 1981 came the ultimate perversion, the attempt through Turkish and Bulgarian proxies to murder the Pope himself. If there are people in Russia who still find this hard to believe, they need only look at the regime's record, then ask themselves: what was the sole country that benefited by the Pope having been stopped from returning to Poland at that time?

As communists secured power in North Korea, Vietnam, Cuba, Cambodia, and Laos, clerics and prelates were attacked and imprisoned in imitation. The biggest wanton success in this sphere was China. What Lenin and Stalin did, Mao Tsetung also undertook. A document published in the Shanghai University journal *Society,* in 1993, estimated that 40 million people died in the vast 1959-61 famine, induced by the crazy policies of the so-called Great Leap Forward.

In the aftermath of the 1989 Tiananmen Square massacre, a number of China's leading intellectuals managed to flee to the West. One was Chen Yizi, a Communist Party member who helped knit together the economic reforms of the 1980s under Dung Xiaoping. Chen settled in America and founded the Center for Modern China, based in Princeton, New Jersey. Chen calculates that from Mao's 1949 takeover of China, through the 1950s landlord and intellectual purges, the Great Leap Forward, the 1966-76 Cultural Revolution, and the prison system, unnatural deaths may have totaled as high as 80 million.

The exiled Cardinal Ignatius Kung of Shanghai has said that when China turned Red in 1949, the Roman Catholic Church there began a long and brave history. "From the beginning, the Communist government wanted to crush religion. The regime systematically and continuously attacked the Roman Catholic Church: levied heavy taxes on the Church, forbade religious instruction in Catholic schools, and restricted or terminated the activities of the lay apostolate, including the Legion of Mary. Chinese bishops, clergy, religious sisters, and Catholic laity were arrested in the tens of thousands. All foreign missionaries, including the Pro-Nuncio, were expelled. Some were imprisoned."

As Bishop of Shanghai, Kung (along with more than 200 priests and lay persons in the Shanghai area) was arrested in 1955 and sentenced to life imprisonment for 'treason'— he refused to cut off his ties and loyalty to the Holy See. He was finally released into house arrest in 1986, and managed to leave China two years later.

That was the force of what was forewarned.

The first apparition to the three Portuguese children, Lucia, Jacinta, and Francisco, who lived near the small village of Fatima, in 1917 on May 13,[1] in a field of the Cova da Iria (Cova means "hollow"), was mysterious and majestic. A young lady, aged about seventeen, bathed in a dazzling light, dressed in white, her head covered with a mantle, and carrying a rosary, told the startled children not to be frightened. *"I come from Heaven,"* she said, speaking only to Lucia, the eldest child. She did not define herself further, but asked the children to return to the Cova at mid-day on the 13th of the month for the next five months, and to say the Rosary.

---

1. The date had had a religious significance particular to Catholic Portugal's devotion to Our Lady for more than five centuries. The late 14th Century enactment—in which Pope Boniface IX, at the request of King John I of Portugal, declared that all Portugal's cathedrals should be dedicated to Our Lady's honor—was read out in Lisbon on a May 13 date.

"Jesus wishes to use you to make me known and loved. He wishes to establish in the world the devotion to my Immaculate Heart," the Lady of light said to Lucia in the second apparition, that of June 13, the feast day of St. Anthony of Lisbon, patron saint of Portugal. Again the Lady declined to say who she was, but the children had guessed it was the Virgin Mary.

Word spread around the district of the distracting events. By mid-day, July 13, a considerable crowd had gathered at the Cova. They heard Lucia cry out: "The Lady is coming."

None but the three children could see the apparition. Several minutes later those in the crowd close to the children saw Lucia go pale as death and heard her cry out in terror. The warning about Russia had been given, and had been preceded by a brief glimpse of the horror of Hell. The Lady asked again that the Rosary be said regularly, and in reply to a question from Lucia, said she would work a public miracle on October 13 so that all who would see it might believe. She would also tell the children whom she was.

Although Lucia[2] had from the outset wanted the children to keep the visions a secret, the younger two had been too excited, and now all Portugal was talking about the matter. Most citizens, it seemed, tended toward a supernatural explanation, for there had been some physical signs: a small, misty cloud had come down at the time and at the site in the Cova where Our Lady was appearing to the children; clouds near the sun had turned blood-red, then pink and yellow. Also, in the face of some severe questioning by the authorities, the childen had maintained, in detail, what they had seen and heard.

By mid-day, October 13, a crowd of 70,000 (some of whom had come to mock) was packed around the Cova. At noon, drizzling rain which had been falling suddenly stopped, and the sun began to shine. "Who are you,

---

2. She was to become a nun, and enter the Carmelite Convent at Coimbra, Portugal. She was present at Fatima on May 13, 1967, when Pope Paul celebrated the 50th anniversary of the first apparition. Francisco and Jacinta, the two other Fatima children, died in 1919 and 1920 respectively, while still young. Lucia is still alive as of May 1995.

and what do you want?" Lucia was heard to ask.

"I am the Lady of the Rosary. Continue to say the Rosary every day. People must amend their lives and ask pardon for their sins. They must not offend Our Lord any more; He is already much offended. I want a chapel built here in my honor."

"Do you want anything more from me?" Lucia asked.

"I want nothing more." She left upward, to the east.

"Look at the sun!" Lucia cried out.

Indeed, the sun appeared to have started to spin like a disc, and to shoot out prismatic rays. A cry went up as one from the huge crowd when the sun, still spinning, appeared to detach itself from the firmament and advance, blood-red, toward the earth, then to be seen, to the relief of all, to have re-attained its proper place in the sky.

This was the marvel Our Lady had promised, the miracle the children had said publicly that she would work, though they had not known the form the miracle was to take. What occurred was noted for the record by a number of people, including the editor of the nationally read secularist newspaper *O Seculo* who, by the gauge of an article published immediately before the October 13 apparition, was one of those who had come to the Cova to mock.

The phenomenon of the October 13, 1917, miracle is something that today we might find hard to accept. Yet, was it any more phenomenal than that which it gave a warning of, and which we all can observe: a Russia which in March 1917, by the true Russian Revolution, had overthrown Tsarism and a millennium of autocracy, to be returned in only eight months to the dictates of a minority regime and become the very words of the Fatima prophecy?

The apparitions ended on that October 13, as Our Lady had in May told the children they would. Had she come back on November 13 in sequence, the Virgin would of course have been beyond the warning of her words. The Marxists' counter-revolution began on November 7 when communist-led apostate army and navy units captured the then capital, Petrograd (formerly St. Petersburg, and to be re-named Leningrad).

The Marxists over-ran Moscow on November 13, which is a timing historians seem to have ignored.

John Paul is indeed a Holy Father who has had "much to suffer." Suffering came early to Karol Wojtyla's life. His mother died when he was only nine. An elder, only brother succumbed to scarlet fever shortly after passing his final doctor's exams, when Karol was aged 13. His one sister, whom he never saw, survived just a day, as we related in Chapter Two. Death took away his father two months before Karol's 21st birthday. Wojtyla, preacher of the strength of familial love, has all his adult life been deprived of the support and sympathy of immediate family members.

All his adult life in Poland was lived under oppressive, dictatorial regimes who deemed the Church a particular enemy. In the first half of his twenties, years which should have been so full of life, he suffered the deadly persecution and peril of German occupation and lost so many of his friends. Two years after he had come to the priesthood in spiritual service to his countrymen, it became the most hazardous profession in Poland, until 1956.

Though the threat of imprisonment was much less, from then on, as Wojtyla's ecclesiastical appointments became more important, so did his sensitivity feel more acutely the plight of his dear Poles forced to live under militant state atheism. When the papacy came, it was accompanied by the devastating loss of his homeland, the first time in more than four and a half centuries a new pope had had to make that sacrifice.

He has been a most Christian pope of peace in a world that mostly resists the reconciliation and redemption of Jesus Christ. Poland, his own beloved land, boldly in 1980-81 became his way of democracy, only to be returned to inhuman Marxism after he was stopped from coming home by a would-be assassin's bullet. He endured a wound of a type every war veteran knows is one of the most painful to suffer, on the sacred ground of his own courtyard, on the anniversary of the particular date with which the Church marks the Fatima apparitions (May 13).

Her victory, the Virgin Mary clearly implied in her prophecy's conclusion, would be in movement with a pope whose Marian devotion was powerfully manifest. Do we not see here another important filiation of John Paul II to

Fatima, for no pope this century, perhaps none ever, has lived his life in such open devotion to Our Lady's Immaculate Heart as Karol Wojtyla, and he comes from that nation where Mary is literally Queen.

The sense of this in him was strong that evening of June 19, 1983, at Jasna Gora when, as we mentioned earlier, he left there a part of the white cassock he was wearing on the day of the 1981 shooting, the part the bullet entered. "O Mother of Jasna Gora, I have come here to say to you once again: 'Totus Tuus!' O Mother, I am completely yours, and all that is mine is yours!

"O Mother! I have been called to serve the universal Church in the Roman chair of Saint Peter. Thinking of this universal service, I repeat constantly: 'Totus Tuus.' "

From Medjugorje—the continuation of Fatima—the Virgin Mary herself responded: "This is my *most* beloved son."

In the early 1980s, it was not hard to see how Fatima could climax. The two colossuses of communism, by declaration and deed intent on the destruction of God's way and will in the world, had closed in upon each other weapons of massive destructive capacity. The Chinese had begun in 1982 to place in hardened, underground silos their first nuclear-armed intercontinental ballistic missiles, and to target them on Russian cities and industries, according to published Western intelligence reports. The Soviet Union, which had its own intercontinental missiles, had been building up its Far East arsenal of SS-20 triple war-headed intermediate range nuclear missiles, the bulk of which bore upon China. In lesser numbers, China had intermediate range, and medium range, missiles, with single nuclear war-heads on each, aimed back at Soviet forces. Two ballistic missile submarines patrolled from Chinese ports. There were armed clashes between the two in 1969 across the Ussuri River, part of the two countries' 4,000-mile common border.

Author George Feifer, perhaps the West's most sentient and honest critic of the Soviet Union, and greatly experienced of that country, wrote in the February 1981 edition of *Harper's* magazine that the Russian people have "a dread of war and fear it will come soon from China."

In March 1984, the Chinese Prime Minister, Zhao Ziyang, publicly told visiting Japanese Prime Minister Yasuhiro Nakasone that "the main threat to China's security comes from the Soviet Union."

And it was during these times that God clearly set out His intentions as regards the Soviet Union. His signs were unequivocal—but did the world see? They began with an extraordinary papal stimulation of Christ's passion and presence in our world, and paralleled the great dates of His Polish Peter's countrymen and women who had stood resolutely against Russian designs. We are now at the exceptional events which intervened upon particular dates of Polish Solidarity and history between John Paul II's writing of his papal bull in November 1982 to proclaim 1983 a Holy Year in remembrance of our redemption by Christ, and the end of that sacred year.

There are three special dates in Solidarity's 1980-81 history: August 31, 1980, the signing of the Gdansk accords between the regime and the striking shipyard workers which won Solidarity its freedoms; November 10, 1980, the legal registration of Solidarity in Poland; December 13, 1981, the imposition of military rule and the removal of Solidarity's democratic rights. Beyond those, the most prominent date in recent Polish history was September 1, 1939, the German invasion and start of the Second World War.

The agreement between the Polish regime and the Vatican for the Pope's second pastoral visit to his homeland, to be undertaken in June 1983, was concluded in the first week of November 1982. The public announcement of the visit was made on Monday, November 8. John Paul thereupon sat down and drafted his papal bull to make 1983 a Holy Year of repentance and reconciliation. He may have had in mind for some time the appropriateness of 1983 for a Holy Year, in its 1950th anniversary of the passion, death, and resurrection of Christ. But as he penned his bull, the irony must have been heavy in John Paul that the regime, which had denied him the right to celebrate with his Poles the 600th anniversary of the installation of *The Black Madonna* painting at Jasna Gora, would now have to have him back in a venerable Holy Year.

On the eve of November 10, 1982, the Kremlin was tense. This was the first anniversary since the re-imposition of absolute dictatorship upon the Polish people—at the Soviet Union leadership's dictate and direction—of the Polish Supreme Court ruling that Solidarity's constitutional statutes would be legally registered. Underground leaders of Solidarity had called for strikes throughout Poland to mark the day. The Kremlin awaited the Poles' reaction. What came on Russian television and radio was the announcement to "the party and the entire Soviet people that Leonid Llyich Brezhnev, General Secretary of the Soviet Communist Party Central Committee and President of the Presidium of the USSR Supreme Soviet, died a sudden death at 8:30 a.m. on November 10, 1982."

The destruction in flight of the South Korean Boeing 747 civilian airliner by the Soviet military in 1983,[3] with the large loss of life, gave the world its sharpest insight that year of Kremlin mentality. The statements of Soviet communism—"the airliner's flight was a deliberate provocation aimed at creating international tension and smearing the Soviet Union"..."this foul spy mission"..."the United States effectively plotted the deaths of the passengers in order to use the incident to discredit the USSR"—showed grossly the contrariness that had become their communist minds, unable to cope with the reality of the regime's deeds. It also showed their inhumanity: no words of apology and atonement came forth from the Kremlin.

But did we especially note the dates on which the airliner was destroyed? In Moscow, it was the evening of August 31, while over the Soviet Sakhalin Island in the Sea of Japan, where the 269 people actually perished in the off-course airliner, it was, due to the time zone differential, early in the morning of September 1.

The Gdansk Agreements between the newly emerged Solidarity and the Polish regime which were signed in 1980, on August 31, achieved for Poles the establishment of new self-governing trade unions to serve the social and

---

3. The editors of *Encyclopedia Britannica* rated the shooting down of the airliner the year's top news story.

material interests of working people, and the guarantee of the essentials of free speech. It was astonishing how that conspicuous, foul Russian act which killed, without apology, those 269 innocent people should have occurred on the Soviet Moscow side on the August 31 Solidarity anniversary, and the on the Soviet Far East side, on the September 1 war anniversary date. The War began in the first hours of September 1, 1939. Those many innocent people in the airliner were killed at 1:20 a.m. local time.

The announcement in Oslo by the Norwegian Nobel Committee that Lech Walesa had been awarded the 1983 Nobel Peace Prize for "his contribution to ensuring workers' rights to establish unions," was made early in October. "Mr. Walesa's contribution was of vital importance in the wider campaign to secure the universal freedom to organize," the Nobel Committee continued. The actual ceremony of presentation of the award was to be made in Oslo in the second week of December.

The Polish regime's defensive declaration that "this is a political award" created uncertainty in the Solidarity leader's mind whether he would be granted a passport to allow him to travel to Norway, and whether, if it were granted, he would be allowed back into Poland—and Walesa therefore decided not to attend the actual award ceremony. Instead, his wife Danuta and their 13-year-old son Bogdan went in his place to Oslo to accept the gold medal and the diploma of the world's most prestigious award.

Thus it came about that Walesa's first act after his physical receipt of the award, from his wife, was to attend a dawn Mass before the shrine of The Black Madonna in Jasna Gora, where he dedicated his Peace Prize to the Queen of Poland and her nation. The date was December 13—anniversary of the re-imposition by martial sword of absolute dictatorship upon Poles.

The events that occurred on those four pivotal Polish dates within the Polish Peter's Holy Year encompass the sudden death of the long-time Soviet dictator, the very public Soviet killing without apology of many innocent people, and lastly the prize of peace given to the Virgin Mary's favor. There would appear to be a prophetic mes-

sage. The sense of God's will appears to be clear: "This
is what I will do, this is why I will do it, but then I will
give the world my Mother's peace."

On May 13, 1984, Fatima's anniversary date, a huge
internal explosion devastated large parts of the Soviet
Union's Severomorsk naval base on the Kola Peninsula
(home of Russia's northern fleet, the country's largest), killing hundreds of people. Western press reports said it was
the biggest Soviet defense disaster since the end of the Second World War.

Yet, we record again, how peaceful was the overthrow
of this powerful and vast atheistic empire, the Soviet
Union. Did we correctly perceive the Lord's anger in the
events of 1982-84 that we have just described? During the
August 1991 coup attempt against Gorbachev, there was
brief machine-gun fire, in Moscow, which killed three people. But that was it. The huge edifice of the Soviet Union
and its atheistic communism just crumbled away in a
peaceful manner under legal signatures.

Did the Queen of Peace bow low before God and ask if
it might be done her way, as a thanksgiving for the faithfulness through torrid trial of the Polish people and the Polish
Pope of whom she is Queen?

When the three children of Fatima first saw Our Lady
in May of 1917, she told them to return to the Cova at noon
on the 13th of each of the next five months, and that on
the 13th of October she would tell them who she was.

Some also believe Our Lady then added: *"And I will
come back here a seventh time."* By implication, that
would be a visitation to take place after the full prophecy
of Fatima had been brought to pass. Is it unreasonable to
speculatively ask if, as he knelt in prolonged private prayer
on May 13, 1991, at the Fatima shrine, Our Lady appeared
to the Holy Father to inform him she was about to remove
the Soviet Union from the map of the world?

We are led naturally to the question: Has then the
prophecy of Fatima been completed in a 1991 climax?

And many probably wish to answer, "Yes,"—were it not
for some facts which appear to be against such affirmation.
The world was warned by the Virgin that the Russia to

come out of 1917 would "spread her errors throughout the world," and we must confront the fact that the most populous country on earth, China, continues under atheistic domination, continues to be a place of persecution of Christians.

The Western world, that most natural abode of Christianity, continues its astonishing retreat from God, and from the sense of sin, and so with no understanding of the generosity of God in the gifts of the Blessed Virgin's victories. The Pope had said, in May 1987, while visting a shrine of St. Michael, near Puglia, Italy: "The Demon is still working in the world. In fact, the evil which exists in it, the disorder which is found in society, the incoherence of man...are not only the consequences of Original sin, but also of the dark and infesting action of Satan."

We must be mindful, too, of the explicit warnings from Garabandal and Medjugorje of a coming chastisement of the world for its many sins and lack of contrition. During the 1960s' apparitions of Our Lady at Garabandal in Spain—the physical evidence of which is overwhelming—the Blessed Virgin spoke (in 1965) during the pontificate of Paul VI to the eldest of the four children who witnessed the apparitions, Conchita Gonzalez, of a coming chastisement to the world. In response to an apprehensive question from Conchita, the Virgin said the chastisement God would deliver would not be a third world war. Our Lady allegedly added: *"There will be two popes after Paul VI."* We are now two popes after Paul VI.

What arose from the Bosnian surrounds of Medjugorje, that special place of Mary's peace, after 1991? A horrific civil war with the genocidal determination of "ethnic cleansing." "A tragedy which in a way seems like the shipwreck of the whole of Europe," was how the Pope described that war in January 1995.

It was three years past the Soviet events of 1991 that Mary spoke her most provocative words about her Pope, from Medjugorje. John Paul was her most beloved son whom she had chosen for *"these times"* (present tense). She added, in that August 1994 declaration, the Fatima designation to her pontiff that he was the one *"who suffers."*

It may be that we can best answer the question we have posed by looking at Russia. Russia, after she had caused much confusion and conflict in the world, would be converted, the Mother of God had promised in 1917. Well, has Russia been converted?

Two images impress—one seen by a few, the other by many: the Soviet Union's Mikhail Gorbachev kneeling at the feet of the Pope in the Vatican, in December 1989, to ask pardon for all the crimes he had committed in his life; and in the blaze of television lights, the Red hammer and sickle flag being lowered from the Kremlin masthead on Christmas Eve 1991.

The great seer of Fatima and carrier of Mary's message, Sr. Lucy, has said, "Yes," Russia has been converted—but then added a seeming "perhaps."

The Blessed Virgin Mary had told Lucia (Lucy), as part of the 1917 prophecy, *"the Holy Father will consecrate Russia to me. Russia will be converted and there will be some peace."* Sr. Lucy, in the October 1992 interview we have referred to previously, was asked if Pope John Paul II had fulfilled Mary's request in 1984, on the feast of the Annunciation, with collegial consecration of Russia?

She seemed to believe that it had, and added: "The fact is that in Russia the communistic, atheistic power prevented the people from carrying out their faith. People now have an individual choice to remain as they are, or convert."

The problem here is which of the two images—the flag of atheistic communism being taken down, or Gorbachev falling to his knees—is more appropriate to the word "conversion?" If tens of millions of Russian people have not followed in Gorbachev's stead, has Russia been converted?

The question is of great importance because the centrality of Russia in the Fatima prophecy is in keeping with its position in world history this century.

What are we to make of the ugliness in Russia today?... the collapse of the health system?...the halving of industrial production the past several years?...the annual three-figure gallop of inflation?...the collapse of the dairy industry?...the sharp increase in drug taking?...the decay of the country's cultural heritage?...the political isolation of President Boris Yeltsin?...the large gap between the small number of *nouveau riche* and the ordinary Russian citizen?...the Mafia-type, well-armed criminal gangs by the thousands, who appear more dominant than the police in big Russian cities (St. Petersburg the worst tragedy)?...the lack of civic and national pride?... the severe fighting in Chechnya in the northern Caucasus, with tank divisions and fighter-bombers involved, and the civilian casualties in the destruction of the capital Grozny? And what of the fact that the leader of the largest single party block of parliamentarians in the State Duma, a neo-fascist and anti-Semite, and probably the most popular politican in Russia today, when he visited an Orthodox church during the December 1993 national elections, had to be shown how to bless himself?

Is this a Holy Russia of Gospel values coming forth?

The Roman Catholic Archbishop of Moscow, Tadeusz Kondrusiewicz, in August 1994, visited the shrine of the Immaculate Heart of Mary in Washington, New Jersey. During Mass there, in his homily, Archbishop Kondrusiewicz thanked Our Lady of Fatima for religious freedom in Russia, and prayed **for** the conversion of Russia. That seems to state the matter most exactly.

If the author may inject a personal note here.... I wrote at some length about the papacy in the early 1980s. I thought I understood reasonably well, through the words and actions of John Paul, the future of his pontificate—that atheistic communism would be lifted from central and eastern Europe upon the vanguard of Poland, that the Soviet Union would break up, and that the Pope would not visit the Holy Land until the Palestinians had rule over a homeland. I also wrote reluctantly that the finale of the Fatima prophecy could bring forth a nuclear war between China and Russia. I even speculated a date for this—May 13, 1987.

It did not matter that symbolically vast forest and bush fires, which destroyed several small towns, burnt each side of the Sino-Soviet border on May 13, 1987. There was no war of nuclear weapons. It is also fair to say that, at the time of writing, I may not have been fully sensitive to the appalling destruction that would take place in such a conflict. I was embarrassed, and, after that, left well enough alone.

I had not heard of the apparitions of the Blessed Virgin at Hrushiv, in the Ukraine, until I picked up *Witness,* an autobiography by Josyp Terelya with Michael H. Brown, published by Faith Publishing Company. When I put the book down at Page 271 I was badly shaken. Terelya, a Catholic activist from the Ukraine, had been a long-term political prisoner of the Soviet Union. In 1972 in his prison cell he was given a vision by Our Lady of a coming war which seemed to involve both Russia and China in imagery that appeared to depict the use of nuclear weapons. He was released early in 1987 under the Gorbachev reforms, just as the Virgin's apparitions at Hrushiv were beginning. Told of them by a nun in April, he made his way to the site. There, a month later, inspired by his own experiences of the Mother of God, he told a crowd what Mary had said to him: *"The world continues on the road of self-will and hedonism. Russia continues to refuse to recognize my Son. Russia rejects true charity and continues to live a demonic existence."* Then Our Lady in regal form in apparition rendered to the crowd gathered around the church of the Blessed Trinity a dire prophecy. She said in part: *"I see a large field in flames and upon it are many nations. There is not even time to dig graves. There is no water. The heavens and the air are on fire."* The date she gave this prophesy on? May 13, 1987.

Pope John Paul was outraged at the Chinese regime's military massacre of many young democrats in Tiananmen Square on June 4, 1989. He gave expression to his anger at this gross offense before the Sunday mid-day Angelus on June 18: "We have been deeply shocked by the news and pictures of the happenings in China, especially by the deaths of so many young people. From the very beginning I have expressed my pain and concern about these tragic events."

John Paul called out to Mary, the Mother of all humanity: "I pray to Mary, Mother of China and Queen of Peace, venerated in the shrine of Sheshan near Shanghai. At this time of such sadness and tragedy, we place in your motherly heart the cry of those who suffer as victims of violence, the pleas of those who hunger and thirst after justice, and the hopes of those who desire their country's good.

"Virgin of Sheshan, Mother of Mercy, obtain light for those who guide the destiny of that great nation, China, so that they may not lack the necessary wisdom in search for the common good, which is based on respect for truth, justice, and freedom."

Six months later, in November 1989, Roman Catholic Bishop Peter Liu Guandong of Yixian, in the Chinese province of Hebei, organized a meeting of Chinese bishops, held in a remote village in Shaanxi province. The ten bishops who attended proclaimed in a document their Catholic faith, and professed full and open communion with Pope John Paul. At the meeting, Bishop Liu was elected president of a permanent committee of the Conference of Chinese Bishops.

Swift was the Chinese regime's response, so hostile is it to God's word and work. Bishop Liu was arrested a mere five days after the meeting. Six months after, on May 21, 1990, Bishop Liu, together with Fr. Xu Zhemin, vicar general of the Baoding diocese, were sentenced to a term of forced labor at a camp near Tangshan. The regime showed its contempt for even the most basic of civil rights—no public or private trial was held for the two churchmen.

On December 15, 1990, the Pope met in Rome with Catholic bishops of Taiwan. He told them: "How can I not be deeply moved to thank God for the shining example offered by bishops, priests, religious, and lay men and women during these years on the Mainland? How can I not be filled with joy at the continuing and ever more frequent reports of loyal communion which come from the leaders and members of those Mainland communities who are always mindful of the Pope in their prayers?

"At the same time there are reports that sadden my heart as Shepherd of the Universal Church. The arrests of bishops, priests, and members of the laity, and various other difficulties, lead one to think that, in spite of some positive signs, there is a long way to go before the beloved Catholic community of China can give full and open expression to its faith and to its ecclesial communion with the Successor of Peter and the Catholic Church spread throughout the world.''

In the years 1991-92, three Catholic bishops died in Chinese jails. One of them was Bishop Peter Fan of Baoding. The Italian Catholic newspaper *Avvenire* said there was evidence that Bishop Fan was tortured before he died, at the age of 85.

Early in 1994, the regime introduced regulations which made it even more difficult for foreign Christian missionaries to teach and preach in China. Foreigners were banned in China from contact with the unofficial church (i.e., any Christian congregation not under the direct rule of the regime, which included of course the Roman Catholic Church which professed the Successor of St. Peter as its head).

No, the signs are that the finale of Fatima has yet to come, which will be when the Virgin weeps for Russia, and for the rest of us.

Chapter 17

What Marx Missed

There stands between God and Marxism one salient word: **love**.

"God is love," Pope John Paul has said many times.

Karl Marx, whose atheistic ideology a century after his death held in bondage one-third of mankind, knew no God, and it is an analogy Wojtyla has noted that Marx, in his major work, *Das Capital*, had no observations to make on human love. The new Pope, by contrast, would declare at a Mass for the College of Cardinals, the day after his election, that his ministry from the outset would be a ministry of love, "for the papacy must always be related to love as the source from which it is nourished."

In hand with love is justice. As John Paul also said in that October of 1978, to one of his first general audiences: "Love 'surpasses' justice, but at the same time it finds its verification in justice. Justice is the fundamental principle of the existence and the coexistence of men and women."

Wojtyla's term for atheistic Marxism is "anti-love." On a supernatural level, that term is from his regard of God as love; on a natural level it is derived from the German-born philosopher's 19th Century writings, and has its denouement in the practices of Marxism. In 1976, as a cardinal in a country that was under a Marxist regime, the future John Paul II spoke of abuses of the individual: "His

138

abuse by production, by consumption, by the state in various totalitarian and crypto-totalitarian countries, under various regimes which start with lofty humane declarations and end up violating elementary human rights. It is this anti-love that divides communities into classes, that incites nations and nationalities to fratricidal clashes, and splits the globe into oppositional 'worlds.' "

Without love, justice, too, is absent. The Pope, speaking at Katowice in the Silesian industrial heartland of Poland on June 20, 1983, said: "The precise meaning of justice and social love is the fullness of the moral order, in connection with the entire social system and, in particular, the system of human work. But if this moral order is missing, injustice takes the place of justice and love is replaced by hatred. It is necessary then that man be truly loved, if his rights are to be fully guaranteed. This is the first and fundamental dimension of social love."

Were a debate between John Paul II and Marx possible on the existence or non-existence of God, John Paul would undoubtedly quickly force Marx to face the issue of love. Historians and biographers tell us that Marx argued that man was an "objective being" and God a "non-objective being." An objective being, Marx said, really existed, but a non-objective being was a non-being, an abstraction. An objective being was dependent on other beings for its existence and open to their casual influence. By contrast, a non-objective being was one who stood in no need of others, was independent of and not casually influenced by them. Thus, according to Marx, if there was a non-objective being (God) it would be the only being in existence. There would be no objective beings. But there are objective beings (man), and so there can be no non-objective being.

That God was perfect existence in Himself and stood in no need of created man, John Paul would agree was a completely valid argument. But the Pope has said many times that God's act of creating first the universe and then man, and giving to man a soul which shared His divine nature for our refuge now and our delight hereafter, was the supreme act of love. God did not have to create us. He "stood in no need of others." Creation was singularly an act of love, John Paul says.

The Pope has long been fastened in fascination to the opening chapters of the Bible's Book of Genesis. No fundamentalist, John Paul believes that religion and science should complement and aid each other. Thus Biblical description of the creation of the universe refers "only to visible reality," he says. By contrast, he is struck by the "psychological precision" of Biblical description. The Pope reads that after God created the universe and its light, after making the earth and its sea, "God was pleased with what He saw." And after making sea creatures and animal life, and then human beings, "God looked at everything He had made, and He was very pleased."

Marx was a man who, in his own words, "embraced materialism." As Lenin said half a century later: "The struggle against religion is the ABC of all materialism, and consequently of Marxism." Even though love and justice are fundamentals of Christ's preachings. "In Poland you cannot struggle against religion in the name of the workers, because, for the Polish worker, religion is wealth, light, way, truth, and life," Cardinal Wojtyla said in 1976 at Nowa Huta. "Man cannot live fully if his gaze is not on God, if he is denied the possibility of saying, 'We want God,' and accomplishing what he means by it. For this reason we must affirm quite clearly that the struggle against religion, against God, is a struggle against man."

Love exists, and how God's love propels conscience was explained by a man whom Wojtyla read in his early years of studying philosophy, St. Augustine of Hippo, a magnificent mind of the early centuries of Christianity: "What is so much not your own self, if you are what you are of another?" In other words, how much of yourself can you claim as fully your own if what you are is the result of something or someone else? From St. Augustine's statement, St. Thomas Aquinas proceeded with the prodigious derivative: "Each thing in the world of nature is what it is only as a function, a product, and a directedness of something else."

Cardinal Wojtyla, in an address at Mainz, in June 1977, after receiving an honorary doctor's degree from the Department of Catholic Theology at Johannes Gutenberg University, said: "The understanding of the human being in his total richness, the understanding of the human being as a personal subject who is capable of self-determination on the basis of self-awareness, who wants to find his fulfill-ment in reference to the transcendental powers of his soul and who strives in different ways toward this goal, is the basic condition for a conscious and creative participation in the current 'struggle for man.' "

The heart of Wojtyla's Christian emotion is the Cross. The Man who walked and talked upon the shores of Galilee was He, the second Person of the Blessed Trinity, God, Who created the universe and passed His hand across the earth to give man life that we could be. This awesome ulti-mate power witnessed in Galilee of Himself: "Learn from me, for I am humble and gentle of heart." This was the nature which surrendered to the scourging at the pillar, the crowning with thorns, the most horrible pain of a six hour-crucifixion. The greatest love that Wojtyla says it is possi-ble for man to know endured man's worst torment so that all men might love in union with His love. John Paul, in homilies, has frequently used the term "the humiliation of the Cross." The fullness of the Son's love moves him almost beyond measure.

Chapter 18

The Return Home

Between the east and west abutments of Europe, at the continent's center, is historic Poland. That is a geographically factual statement. But, in 1983, would any political scholar in the West, or in the East perhaps, have deemed that of Poland in an ideological sense?

Pope John Paul II, that most insightful and intelligent of men, did, on June 17, 1983, and in a setting that could not have been more dramatic: inside the high ceiling chamber of Warsaw's neo-classical Belweder Palace, standing four yards across from an erect, nervous General Wojciech Jaruzelski, the first time the Pope had been face to face with the Communist Party chief and martial law enforcer.

"I ardently desire," John Paul said with studied directness, "that Poland may have her proper place among the nations of Europe—between the East and the West."

The Pope's words did not gain any headlines. Indeed, they were little reported in Western Europe and North America's principal newspapers and news magazines. Was this because his words were empty rhetoric which did not face the reality of Poland's membership in the communist Soviet bloc? But surely wouldn't John Paul, of all people, have known the ideological encumbrance and Soviet domination of his homeland? After all, did he not carry the marks of it on his body?

Yes, we in the West underestimated this man. His is an intellectual resource and resolution which had conceived a breathtaking endeavor that a President Ronald Reagan or a Prime Minister Margaret Thatcher would never have had the wit in a hundred years to attempt.

An immense danger lay upon humanity—all humanity—a peril which made the Pontiff see the hour of death on the horizon of our history. And 18 months later, he described the particular point from where that peril came: he said, at Christmas 1984, that "atheism has brought to the world the permanent threat of nuclear war." Given the mentality and morals of the nuclear protagonists at that time, a substantial reduction in atomic armaments was unlikely to be our relief. Therefore, if what was on the horizon and drawing much closer each day could not from without be recessed and returned to a distance, then it had to be done from within. And this was done in central and eastern Europe by overcoming the inertia and sloth of the dictated peoples with an image of themselves that is noble and uplifting. This returns the sense of their human dignity and rights, and galvanizes them to seek what is natural, to express the true selves they have reverted to, a mold and mood removed of Marxism.

Should that have been believed implausible in the 1983 European situation, in the European spring of 1981, John Paul just may have come within pistol shot wounds of pulling it off.

His thinking is the product of a great generosity of spirit and understanding of humanity. As we have observed in this book, through the Pope's own words, he believes singularly in the capacity of a person to look inside himself or herself for the truth, and that the truth has a creative union with freedom which is unbreakable. These are values communism would extinguish, and Christianity would distinguish. Naturally, the Vicar of Christ would assert and encourage those values where their need was greatest—and they were worse violated within the half of Europe possessed by Soviet communism.

When Providence drew Karol Wojtyla forth from Poland to the seat of St. Peter, his mind would return to the Eastern conflict of Christianity and communism as readily as it would return to his homeland—and it would do so as the nuclear forces of the East and West made, in their confrontation, a possible conclusion to humanity.

The violation of Poland's borders spurred World War II. Of all the national victims of that six-year conflict, none suffered more than Poland. And through four decades of the War's aftermath it was within Polish society that the forces of good and evil fought their most intense moral and ideological battle. No national people practice a stronger Catholicism than the Poles, while the state and its potent apparatuses were the activity of satraps (subordinate rulers) of Soviet Marxists still determined for the obliteration of Christianity.

After the initial heavy blow of the loss of dearest Poland, the new Pope came to see his Polish and Slav communion as a sign of God's wish and will to give a unique advantage for John Paul to attempt fundamental change in central and eastern Europe. That would bring forth the ascendancy of the common good, and brake the precipitation to a nuclear arms catastrophe. That Poland was the obvious point in Eastern Europe to apply the particular pressure of this historic endeavor was in empathy with the country's historic proportions.

It is there in the text of the Pope's Belweder Palace address given those few steps across from General Jaruzelski, the speech that was carried nationwide on Polish television, the sensational confrontation that drew to Warsaw so many foreign journalists.

But now, in June 1983, John Paul had it all in front of him again. Now, in the political circumstances changed so very considerably from those of May 1981, which should have been the time of his second home-coming, he had to put emphasis on the need for dialogue.

The Apostolic See devoted so many of its efforts to the cause of peace in today's world, the Pope told the General in their stately setting. Those efforts were very numerous and at the same time generally known; it would be difficult at the moment to mention them in detail. "I will mention only the initiative of the Pontifical Academy of Sciences in 1981. Eminent specialists in the scientific disciplines such as physics, biology, genetics, and medicine drew up a memorandum on the foreseeable consequences of the use of atomic weapons." (This was the report which estimated that most of our planet's major cities could be destroyed by a mere 200 nuclear bombs. East and West possessed more than 100 times that many bombs.)

John Paul then reminded the General and all listening of his January 1, 1983, *World Day of Peace* message, and repeated in part what he had written in that message: "People are finally capable of overcoming divisions, conflicts of interest, even if the oppositions would seem radical ones...if they believe in the virtue of dialogue. Dialogue for peace must be established in order to resolve social conflicts, in order to seek the common good."

Even so, he would not step back from his great challenge: "I ardently desire that Poland may always have her proper place among the nations of Europe—between the East and the West. I ardently desire the recreation of conditions of 'good cooperation' with all the Western nations on our continent, as well as in the Americas."

Pope John Paul did succeed by his visit in having martial law abolished in Poland (it had been suspended the previous December), a month after he had returned to the Vatican. The law disappeared on July 22, Poland's so-called national day (it is, in fact, little more than the anniversary of the country's first, enforced communist constitution). But as Roger Boyes had written from Warsaw in *The Times* of London three days previously: "The abolition of martial law has little practical import for ordinary Poles. Solidarity has been crushed as a mass movement, most platforms of intellectual opposition have been banned or purged, the penal code has been tightened, censorship is stiffer, government powers have been extended, the Party and state administration has been thinned out, and some economic and education reforms have been introduced which may or may not prove effective. Martial law has served its purpose and can now go."[1]

---

1. Between the Pope's return to Rome and the abolition of martial law the Kremlin had rendered to Jaruzelski an Order of Lenin, the USSR's highest civilian award. In October 1985, between 66 percent (the banned Solidarity's estimate) and 79 percent (the regime's claimed number) of adult Poles voted in the country's first national election since 1980. For the 460 seats in Parliament only candidates approved by the Communist Party were permitted to be elected.

An amnesty law was passed at the same time, and in mid-August the regime announced that, during the previous three weeks, it had released from Polish jails 400 political prisoners, making clear that the regime had been holding more such prisoners than it had claimed in December 1982.[2] A number of top Solidarity activists remained in confinement. Then a few days later the regime turned around and dissolved the Polish Writers' Union, claiming it was a center of anti-socialist activity, leaving the Church the only legal instrument of opposition.

The first task of John Paul II, when he stepped onto the soil of his homeland for the second time as Pope, was to revive the spirits of his countrymen. He had seen fifteen years previously the appalling apathy the Czech people had fallen into after their Prague spring had been iced over by the Soviet invaders. But political and religious sensibilities were acute. There was required of him a rigorous intellectual finesse the like of which may not have confronted any other modern-day statesman.

On the day before his departure in a brief, cautious Vatican speech he had given thanks to the communist-military leadership for allowing him to undertake his second papal pilgrimage. Later in the same day the Soviet dictator and particular opponent of the Pope, Yuri Andropov, had said in the Kremlin that the "reformist danger" in Poland was past and would not return, provided Warsaw was vigilant and did not relax its grip. The next day, as John Paul left for Warsaw, Andropov and Andrei Gromyko made their especial speeches before the Supreme Soviet. Understandably, the people of Poland waited for the Pope's Alitalia aircraft with uncertainty.

Pope John Paul regained his birthright with a kiss of its soil on June 16, 1983. "The kiss placed on the soil of Poland has a particular meaning for me. It is like a kiss placed on the hands of a mother, for the homeland is our earthly mother. She is a mother who has suffered much and who ever suffers anew. Therefore she also has a right to

---

2. In 1984, exactly the same thing was seen to have happened, when in July-August the regime released 652 political prisoners, including eleven key Solidarity leaders.

a special love. Peace be to you Poland, my homeland.''

As his aircraft from Rome had neared Warsaw he had been asked by accompanying journalists how he felt to be going home? John Paul's response had been one word of English: "Myself."

His face, after the kiss of his soil, was tense with emotion almost to distress, a profile vividly captured in the photograph which centered *The Times* of London's June 17 edition's front page. This was his country. These were his people. Their one and a half years' of suffering had been his.

The strength to bear his suffering he drew from their strength in their suffering: "I ask those who are suffering to be particularly close to me. I ask this in the name of Christ's words— *I was sick and you visited me. I was in prison and you came to me.'* I myself am not able to visit all the sick, the imprisoned, the suffering, but I ask them to be close to me in spirit, to sustain me as they always do."

The authorities had deliberately restricted to a small crowd those people actually allowed into the airport's confines to listen to John Paul's brief speech. Now as he was driven standing into the center of Warsaw in a glass-enclosed, white popemobile, people packed twelve deep at the curbsides. Some men were openly weeping. There were some arms and fingers raised in the victory "V" sign, and some shouts of "Solidarity!" and "Walesa!" What had been so many faces without smiles as Poles gathered there in the hours before his arrival now became an emotional response to his presence.

He went first to the red brick, gothic Basilica of St. John, descended to the cathedral's underground crypt to pray in front of Cardinal Stefan Wyszynski's tomb, then ascended to celebrate his first Mass and deliver his first homily, in front of a crammed congregation. The first words of that first sermon were of the Son of God in the mystery of the Redemption, of His "humiliation" in death on the Cross, then His "exaltation" through the Resurrection. It was as if John Paul was drawing an allegorical observation of present-day Poland and his hope for his country's future.

The events of the Redemption, he went on, had passed into history, and the world was separated from them by

1950 years. "But the redemption of the world continues inexhaustibly and is always available anew to each person, to every man and woman. In a special way it is available to those who suffer, and perhaps suffer more intensely because they cannot fully perceive the meaning of their own suffering and, even more, the meaning of their own existence." Deftly, sublimely, he put the vast majority of Poles above their atheistic rulers, and showed the inspiration he could return to them through their own spirituality.

"Let us allow ourselves to be caught up in the mystery of the Redemption!" he continued. "We all stand beneath the Cross. All humanity stands continually beneath the Cross. Together with all my compatriots, especially with those who are most acutely tasting the bitterness of disappointment, humiliation, suffering, of being deprived of their freedom, of being wronged, of having their dignity trampled upon, I stand beneath the Cross of Christ, to celebrate on Polish soil the extraordinary jubilee of the Year of the Redemption." There, at its most emphatic, was the political message inside the religious ministration.

The first steps of his pilgrimage, John Paul told the congregation, had been to the tomb of the great Primate, Cardinal Wyszynski. "I was not able to come to Warsaw for his funeral, on May 31, 1981, because of the attempt on my life on May 13." Publicly, for the first time, he had brought the two events together, and had waited until he was in Poland to mark their relationship. But he said no more of it during the sermon. Rather, he gave thanks that "in the difficult period of our history after the Second World War," Poland had been given this Primate—"this intrepid servant of the Church and of the homeland." And suddenly the Pope was quoting the deceased cardinal, his friend, and it was several seconds before the congregation realized from where the Pope was taking the Primate's words. When they did there was a huge burst of applause—this in a church—for the words were of *Notes from Prison,* a diary the cardinal kept during his 1953-56 years in prison, and later published. All in the cathedral knew that John Paul's restatements were nothing about the period of the 1950s.

The Pope strengthened his tribute to the Primate: "He was strong in his faith in Christ, that cornerstone of salvation of each person, of humanity, of the nation. He did everything that this cornerstone might not be rejected by the people of our time, but rather might be reconsolidated as the foundation of the spiritual structure of the modern and future generations. Like the Apostle Paul, the late Primate, too, preached Christ crucified, who is the power of God and the wisdom of God before a world that in every age seeks other powers and other forms of wisdom.''

Again he quoted *Notes from Prison:* "Sadness, which makes the soul tremble, is the plowing of the land before the new sowing.''

Stefan Wyszynski ever stood beneath the Cross of Christ together with Mary, the Pope continued. "In her regard, he felt like the Apostle John, like an adopted son. In this giving without reserve, he found his own spiritual freedom; yet, he was a free man, and he taught us, his compatriots, true freedom. He was a tireless herald of the dignity of every person and of the good name of Poland among the nations of Europe and the world. Divine Providence spared him the sad events associated with the date of December 13, 1981.'' There was more loud applause from the congregation.

In giving thanks to the most Blessed Trinity for the great service of the Primate, John Paul went on: "Let us beg the King of Ages that nothing may destroy this deep foundation that it was given to him to establish in the soul of the people of God throughout the land of Poland.'' The Pope turned portentously and went down from the pulpit.

In its instruction and inspiration, in the deliberate mix of the deft and the direct, in the building of his presence upon the late, resolute Primate's foundation of freedom, John Paul's sermon was an extraordinary performance, and harbinger of his eight-day tour.

Immediately after the Mass it was clear that people were taking courage from what he was saying. A crowd of more than 10,000, and of all ages, marched from the cathedral through Warsaw with chants of freedom and shouts that the Pope was with them. They dispersed good-naturedly with a chorus of "O God Who Has Protected Poland"—a nationalist hymn and a signature of Solidarity—after being stopped from reaching the Communist Party central committee headquarters by hundreds of militiamen.

There was a poignant moment the next morning at the Church of the Capuchins when the Pope recognized the mother of 18-year-old Grzegorz Przemyk of Warsaw, a Solidarity supporter who had been beaten to death by several militiamen the previous month. The Pope came across to her, spoke to her softly, kissed her cheek.

That evening, at a Mass before one million people packed in and around Warsaw's huge Tenth Anniversary soccer stadium, he stood wearing a golden chasuble and gold miter beneath a 40-foot tall white crucifix and compellingly reminded the West of particular Polish sacrifices: "From this city Warsaw, the capital of the nation and of the state that, at the cost of the greatest sacrifices, fought for the good cause during the last World War, I wish to remind everyone that Poland's right to sovereignty and also to correct development in the cultural, social, and economic fields appeals to the consciences of many people and many societies in the world. As an ally, Poland maintained to the very end, indeed abundantly, the commitments she assumed in the terrible experiences of the years 1939-45. The fate of Poland in 1983 cannot be a matter of indifference to the nations of the world, especially those of Europe and America."

At his first public function at the monastery of Jasna Gora, the next day, in an address to a large pilgrimage from Szczecin-Kamien, the Pope reminded East Europeans that Christ had to be the center of any struggle for freedom: "The whole world was amazed in 1980 when the Polish worker stood up for himself with the Gospel in his hand and a prayer on his lips. Only the person who has been renewed within, for whom the supreme criterion is the complete teaching about man, can in peace and with courage build up a new world."

Pope John Paul had said before he departed from Rome that the principal religious reason for his coming presence in Poland would be to join in the 600th year anniversary celebrations of the installation (at the then recently founded Jasna Gora monastery, above Czestochowa) of *The Black Madonna,* the dark-hued portrait of the Virgin Mary and her child, the Christ. The portrait is Poland's holiest icon, and revered symbol of the country's culture and nationalism. The actual year of the icon's installation was 1382, and all knew why, 600 years later, the Pope had been unable to come from Rome in 1982.

Even after the formal agreement for the Pope to visit, there had remained a lingering doubt that the pilgrimage would take place. That doubt had hardened in January 1983, when a return of repressive measures in Poland[3] led John Paul to pray publicly in the Vatican to Our Lady of Czestochowa: "To you I entrust if and how the visit will take place." All waited, as a consequence, to see if he would utter *that* word, the great word of August 1980 and the ensuing sixteen months of vibrant freedom. The Pope waited too, waited for Czestochowa, and for the vast, especial gathering before the monastery of young Poles, with whom he has such affinity and for whom he has such hope.

Before him were three-quarters of a million youthful, exuberant people, many holding aloft banners bearing the name of the outlawed trade union federation, *that* name. The Pope began his address with a buoyant avowal of the Virgin Mary's Queenship: "I am happy that we are here together, before the Mother of our nation. I am happy because, together with you, dear young friends, I can meditate on the concise and yet so rich content of the call of Jasna Gora. As we say and sing the words of the hymn, 'Mary, Queen of Poland, I am near you, I remember you, I watch,' we do not only bear witness to the spiritual presence of the Mother of God amongst the generations living on Polish soil. These words also prove that we believe in the love which surrounds us constantly. This love was born at the foot of the Cross, when Christ entrusted to Mary His disciple John: *'Behold your son.'* We believe that, in that one man, Christ entrusted to her every human being, and at the same time awoke in her heart a love which is a maternal reflection of His own redemptive love.

"We believe that we are loved by this love, surrounded by it, that is, by the love of God, which was revealed in

---

3. Parallel to this, state authorities conducted an intimidating campaign against Western press representatives in Poland and, in circumstances of invented nastiness, expelled the United Press International reporter Ruth Gruber.

the Redemption, and by the love of Christ, who accomplished this Redemption by means of the Cross, and finally by the love of the Mother who stood beneath the Cross and who, from the heart of her Son, accepted into her heart every human being.

"The words, 'I am near you, I remember you, I watch,' are in fact at the same time a confession of love, with which we desire to correspond to the love with which we have been eternally loved. Our Lady of Jasna Gora is the teacher of true love for all. And this is particularly important for you, dear young people. In you, in fact, is decided that form of love which all of your life will have and, through you, human life on Polish soil: the matrimonial, family, social, and national form—but also the priestly, religious, and missionary one. Every life is determined and evaluated by the interior form of love. I watch! How beautiful it is that this word is found in the call of Jasna Gora." He was now approaching another word, *that* word.

"My dear friends! It is up to you to put up a firm barrier against immorality, a barrier—I say—to those social vices, which I will not here call by name but which you yourselves are perfectly aware of. You must demand this of yourselves, even if others do not demand it of you. Today when we are fighting for the future form of our social life, remember that this form depends on what people will be like. Therefore: watch!"

Then came the word. " 'I watch' also means: I see another. I do not close in on myself, in a narrow search for my own interests, my own judgments. 'I watch' means: love of neighbor; it means: fundamental inter-human solidarity." Cheers and applause burst upon the Pope, and came again, wave after wave. A canopy of up-raised arms with fingers of V for victory set itself and held itself above the vast crowd.

John Paul, never one to do things by halves, continued when he was able: "Before the Mother of Jasna Gora, I wish to give thanks for all the proofs of this solidarity." Pandemonium! Cheers and shouts.

Then, again when he was able, the Pope put his spoken seal on the democracy and decency which Solidarity had brought to Poland: "May this good thing, which appeared in so many places and so many ways, never cease on Polish soil." It was a speech which moved beautifully from exhaltation to exclamation, and which urged upon Polish youth the solidarity which begot Solidarity.

The regime in Warsaw was now desparately trying to claw back some of the immense popularity for the events of 1980-81 that the Pope had rekindled in the public's hearts by his forceful speeches. Deputy Prime Minister Mieczyslaw Rakowski, said: "He who addresses youth should remember that millions of young people learn and work honestly and relate their future to socialism, want more socialism in their lives...." Foreign journalists accompanying the Pope hurried Rakowski's words over the wires to their editors at home. Poles sat back with a quiet smile, in fact it was quite a large smile. The deputy prime minister's statement came just before the most forceful of all John Paul's pilgrimage speeches on the Solidarity era.

The people of the Silesian coal-mining region (which is in the south of the country) are the most conservative of Poles. They were the last to accept Solidarity in 1980, but, having made their acceptance, became fiercely loyal to the trade union federation. Their region is also the industrial—and thus workers'—heartland of Poland. Their main city is steel-producing Katowice, and it was here on June 20, that John Paul spoke before one and a quarter million at an open air Mass. "When at work, we mutually greet each other with the expression *'Szczesc Boze'* (May God help you). We express in this way our good will toward our neighbor who is working, and, at the same time, we put his work in the hands of God the Creator, God the Redeemer. Human work really is at the heart of all social life. Through it justice and social love are formed, if the whole working sector is governed by a just moral order. But if this order is missing, injustice takes the place of justice and love is replaced by hatred.

"The entire world has followed and continues to follow with emotion the events that took place in Poland from August 1980." Thunderous applause met the marking of the date. "The thing that, in a special way, gave public opinion cause to reflect was the fact that, in these events, it was a question, above all, of the moral order itself in relation to human work, and not only the question of an increase in salary. Also striking was the fact that these events were free from violence, that no one was killed or wounded by them." The Pontiff's implicit contrast with the deaths of seven Katowice miners during clashes with militiamen after the imposition of martial law in December 1981 drew an audible, emotional response from the crowd (more so, perhaps, because relatives of the victims had been invited to sit close to the podium from where the Pope was speaking).

"The experience of history teaches that trade unions are an indispensable element of social life, especially in modern industrialized societies. They are a mouthpiece for the just rights of working people. It was in this spirit that I spoke in January 1981, during an audience granted in the Vatican to the delegation of Solidarnosc"—applause and cheering roared to the podium and went on and on. He had said it, not just lower case "s" but **it**.[4] The crowd burst into a chorus of the traditional song *"Sto Lat"* (May You Live a Hundred Years). The Pope finally had to motion for silence. "I am still alive and would like to go on with my speech," he said in good humor.

"So then, beloved, the discussion that has been going on in Poland in recent years has a deep moral sense. It cannot be resolved in any other way than through a true dialogue between the authorities and society. The bishops of Poland, many times during this period, have called for such a dialogue."

Now the Pope had come to Cracow, the Cracow whose every stone and every brick was dear to him—home.

He arrived to the reverberating boom of the Zygmunt, a large bell rung from Wawel Hill only on very special occasions. The roads over which he came to the archbishop's residence were covered with flowers and blossoms. His Cracovians pressed in on all sides, and pastor and parishioners reciprocated their intimate delight in each other.

---

4. And Solidarnosc, not Solidarity, was how it was spelled in the English translation by Vatican press officials for Western journalists following the Pope in Poland.

John Paul entered the residence that had been his for fifteen years, but they called him out onto a second floor balcony. "I am so happy to be home a second time," he shouted down to them all. "Come a third time," they shouted back.

Over on the edge of the city, preparations in Blonie Park meadow were nearly complete to receive two million people—almost three times the population of Cracow—the next day, Wednesday, June 22, for John Paul's open air Mass and sermon. This celebration would be personally and particularly *his*. In this same meadow, four years before, he had made that emotional farewell to Cracow and Poland at the end of his 1979 pilgrimage, had pleaded with his people to be strong in their faith, and then had lifted his eyes for one last look at his cherished city. This was where the self of him was strongest.

When they came to Blonie Park meadow the following morning, the two million people to make the largest congregation of his tour, all expected to hear again those sentiments of four years ago, shaped to the post-Solidarity situation. John Paul II surprised them. Not only did he not do the expected, he did what had never been done before—in an insight of what might have been in May-June 1981, and by implication what might still be. And when he had finished, the noises that came out of Warsaw showed that the Soviet satraps there had been shaken silly. From Moscow came silence, deafening by its muteness.

John Paul began his sermon by giving glory to "the Lord who is our Shepherd: He is the Good Shepherd of His flock. He said it about Himself in the Gospel. We know that He seeks above all to preserve the unity of His flock. On the last day of my pilgrimage in union with the jubilee of Jasna Gora, here in Cracow, my dear compatriots, I wish, together with you, to give voice to the wonderful presence of the Good Shepherd in the midst of all the generations that have lived on Polish soil and have left, here in Cracow, a unique expression of their Polish and Christian identity."

Then he was formally welcoming and greeting all "my dear compatriots" present, then Polish cardinals and bishops, several cardinals from abroad, then all the clergy of the archdiocese, then priests who had come from all the other parts of Poland.

They were a special audience, for "today, in fact, I am able to fulfill a special service: to raise to the altars through beatification some servants of God." There were startled murmurings from the crowd. Ceremonies of beatification —the last step before sainthood—traditionally are conducted in the Vatican. Never in the seven centuries of Cracovian Catholicism had such a ceremony been undertaken in this city. John Paul himself went on to admit: "Normally this kind of service takes place in Rome. Nevertheless, it has been my ardent desire that my pilgrimage to the homeland, in conjunction with the jubilee of Jasna Gora, should also become an opportune occasion to raise to the altars certain servants of God whose path to sanctity is linked with this land and this nation."

But he kept everyone in suspense for several minutes as to who these individuals to be accorded such honor by the Church were, as rather he expounded generally on the act of beatification. Then he gave the names: Father Rafal Kalinowski and Brother Albert Chmielowski.

The crowd was shock still. It knew the history of the two men. They were Polish clergymen—who had joined with Poles in 1863 in a general uprising against Russian rule of Poland.

"The Lord Jesus said, *'Greater love has no man than this, that a man lay down his life for his friends.'* This giving of one's life for one's friends, for one's compatriots, was evidenced in 1863," the Pope said. "Both Father Rafal and Brother Albert were inspired by heroic love of the homeland."

John Paul was delivering the speech in which, by the precedent of 1979, Poles expected him to give most intimately of himself. He was proceeding in that speech in signal recognition of, and Church reward for, two religious orders' members who had confronted regnant St. Petersburg with their fellow Poles en masse.

Had the Polish priest and Pope, John Paul II, not been bloodily stopped from coming back to Poland in 1981, he might well have been part of a general uprising against Soviet domination of his countrymen, and possibly more. John Paul at Gniezno, Poland, in June 1979, had, as we depicted in Chapter 14, spoken in unequivocal words a wisdom that Providence had brought forth a Polish and Slav pope with a particular Christian destiny in Eastern Europe. Allied to that was his belief, broad upon his mind, that if Christian principles were not returned to the eastern half of the European continent, man could pass to the fate of nuclear extermination.

John Paul would have known that, given the nature of the Soviet beast, such personal and papal endeavor would ultimately mean a show-down with the anti-Christian Kremlin. Conditions for that show-down came surprisingly quickly, and were at their most propitious in the spring of 1981. Had it begun in the Pope's presence in Warsaw, its eventual outcome might have been dependent on events in neighboring countries. In that observation, there is another parallel with the 1863 uprising: peoples of Lithuania, the Ukraine, and later Latvia joined in the rebellion against Russian rule.

One hundred and eighteen years later, these same people were no more inclined to Soviet rule. The Czech and Hungarian peoples, southern neighbors of the Poles, were of the same suasion. "This Pope, in whose heart is deeply engraved the history of his own nation from its very beginning and also the history of brother peoples and the neighboring peoples," John Paul had said during his 1979 Gniezno speech. When he had broken from his Blonie Park meadow address to introduce Church dignitaries seated behind him before beginning the service of beatification, two of the several cardinals he had welcomed were from Czechoslovakia and Hungary. Czech volunteers had fought in the ranks of the Polish insurgents during the 1863 uprising.

Would the center of the Soviet empire hold if its Baltic Sea-Black Sea circumference, predominantly Catholic, in whose midst would have stood an East European Pope, collapsed about it? What if the competing and Moslem nationalities of the Asian half of the USSR saw the main chance?

John Paul had, to an extent, been preparing his pilgrimage audiences for what he would say to the great Cracow gathering; several times his speeches had been threaded with military themes. At his first outdoor Mass, on June 17, at the Tenth Anniversary stadium in Warsaw, the Pope had reminded those many present that "in the year 1983, there is gloriously highlighted a historic date of three hundred years ago: the relief of Vienna, the victory of Vienna! This is the anniversary that unites us all, the Poles and also our neighbors to the south and to the west."

As he had closed the Jasna Gora ceremonies, on June 19, he referred to the year 1655 when Jasna Gora had resisted the pressure of the invading Swedish armies "from when subsequently the entire homeland was freed from the invaders." Then at Wroclaw, in the Lower Silesia, on June 21, again before one million people, he had reached right back to the first half of the 13th Century and to the memory of a great Silesian son, Henry the Pious, who, in opposition to the invading Tartars, fell near Legnica. "The Tartars had penetrated with their armed troops far into the west, through the whole of the Polish territory. Henry the Pious fell on the field of battle, but the Tartars went no further toward the west. Indeed, they retreated toward the east, and thus the lands of the Piasts were freed from their yoke."

The beatification of Father Rafal Kalinowski emphatically placed the aura of 1863 on the Polish era of the 1980s, for Father Rafal had become known in contemporary Poland as "the Solidarity saint." (The uprising succumbed in 1864, principally because unity between propertied classes and the peasantry did not coagulate. Rafal Kalinowski had been one of the leaders of the insurrection, and after his capture by the Tsarist army, a sentence of death was commuted to ten years hard labor and exile in Siberia. Eventually he returned to Poland and entered the novitiate of the Carmelite Order, and in his preachings kept alive the vision of an independent Poland.)

The Pope's decision to beatify Brother Albert Chmielowski may have part of its significance in the penalty Brother Albert suffered for his part in the insurrection— mutilation (he lost a leg). Is there a contemporary Pole who has suffered serious physical wounds for resisting Russian (Soviet) rule over his country? Of course, the Pope. Was beatification of Brother Albert, John Paul's masterly and majestic way of informing the killers in the Kremlin he was well aware of what they had been about? (Albert Chmielowski was first a painter. When he had recovered from the

Bibliography

BLAZYNSKI, George. *John Paul II: A Man from Krakow.* Weidenfeld and Nicolson.

BOSCO, Father Teresio. *Saint Maximilian Kolbe.* A.C.T.S. Publications, Melbourne.

CRAIG, Mary. *Man from a Far Country.* Hodder and Stoughton.

de ROECK, Jef. *The Man from Poland,* (translated by Jack Riede). Methuen.

DEWAR, Diana. *Saint of Auschwitz, the Story of Maksymilian Kolbe.* Darton, Longman and Todd, London.

FONTANA LIBRARY. *The Varieties of Religious Experience.* (The Gifford Lectures, 1901-02).

FROSSARD, Andre. "Be Not Afraid!" Andre Frossard in Conversation with John Paul II. Bodley Head.

GARAUDY, Roger. *Marxism in the 20th Century,* (translated by Rene Hague). Collins.

GILBERT, Martin. *Winston S. Churchill Volume IV* and *Volume V.* Heinemann, London.

GRENET, Paul. *Thomism, An Introduction,* (translated by James F. Ross). Harper and Row.

HEBBLETHWAITE, Peter. *Year of Three Popes.* Collins.

KAROLAK, Tadeusz. *John Paul II: The Pope from Poland,* (translated by David Evans). Interpress Publishers, Warsaw.

KESTON COLLEGE. *Religion in Communist Lands,* Vol. 9 Nos. 1-2.

KUNG, Hans. *Does God Exist?* Doubleday.

LAURENTIN, René and RUPCIC, Ljudevit. *Is the Virgin Mary Appearing at Medjugorje?* The Word Among Us Press.

LONGFORD (Lord). *Pope John Paul II.* Michael Joseph-Rainbird.

MALINSKI, Father Mieczyslaw. *Pope John Paul II: The Life of My Friend Karol Wojtyla.* Burns and Oates.

NICHOLS, Peter. *The Pope's Divisions: the Roman Catholic Church Today.* Faber and Faber.

ORAM, James. *The People's Pope.* Bay Books, Sydney.

PIEPER, Josef. *Introduction to Thomas Aquinas,* (translated by Richard and Clara Winston). Faber and Faber.

SCHOPFLIN, George. *Politics in Eastern Europe 1945-92.* Blackwell, Oxford.

SOLOVYOV, Vladimir and KLEPIKOVA, Elena. *Boris Yeltsin.* G. P. Putnam's Sons, New York.

STRUVE, Nikita. *Christians in Contemporary Russia,* (translated by Lancelot Sheppard and A. Manson). Harvill Press, London.

TERELYA, Josyp and BROWN, Michael H. *Witness.* Faith Publishing Company, Milford.

THOMPSON, Colin P. *The Poet and the Mystic; A Study of the Cantico Espiritual of San Juan de la Cruz.* Oxford University Press.

VON RAUCH, Georg. *A History of Soviet Russia,* (translated by Peter and Annette Jacobsohn). Frederick A. Praeger, New York.

WANDYCZ, Piotr. *A History of East Central Europe, Volume VII (The Lands of Partitioned Poland, 1795-1918).* University of Washington Press.

WHALE, John (ed). *The Pope from Poland: An Assessment.* Fount.

Faith Publishing Company

Faith Publishing Company has been organized as a service for the publishing and distribution of materials that reflect Christian values, and in particular the teachings of the Catholic Church.

It is dedicated to publication of only those materials that reflect such values.

Faith Publishing Company also publishes books for The Riehle Foundation. The Foundation is a non-profit, tax-exempt producer and distributor of Catholic books and materials worldwide, and also supplies hospital and prison ministries, churches and mission organizations.

For more information on the publications of Faith Publishing Company, contact:

Faith Publishing Company
P.O. BOX 237
MILFORD, OHIO 45150